The College Administrator's
SURVIVAL GUIDE

The College Administrator's
SURVIVAL GUIDE

C. K. Gunsalus

HARVARD UNIVERSITY PRESS
Cambridge, Massachusetts
London, England
2006

Library of Congress Cataloging-in-Publication Data
Gunsalus, C. K.
    The college administrator's survival guide / C. K. Gunsalus.
        p.   cm.
    Includes bibliographical references and index.
    ISBN 13: 978-0-674-02315-4 (alk. paper)
    ISBN 10: 0-674-02315-3 (alk. paper)
    1. College personnel management—United States.
    2. Conflict management—United States.   I. Title.

    LB2331.68.G86   2006
    378.1'11—dc22   2006043355

To Donald L. Bitzer and Larry R. Faulkner

who introduced me to the satisfaction of doing work
in which I can believe and showed me how to work
from principles and for the best interests of the institution

Contents

The College Administrator's
SURVIVAL GUIDE

Introduction

One of the most puzzling aspects of higher education is that its front-line leaders are almost always selected for qualities other than an ability to run complex organizations. In fact, it is often seen as virtually disqualifying for a candidate to express anything but the most grudging willingness to assume administrative responsibilities. At least on the surface, the path to becoming a leader in an academic environment is to affect a lack of interest in and preparation for the job.

And yet colleges and universities are among the most complicated organizations around—and they present unique challenges for administrators. The central factor of an academic environment is that it contains what was trendy some years back to call "knowledge workers." These are people with highly specialized expertise, who are not usually susceptible to being managed in the traditional sense of the word. Their attitude toward administrators is often one of disdain: a commonly heard quip asserts that an academic who takes on an administrative role loses twenty I.Q. points. A university is about as far as it is possible to get from the command-and-control hierarchy of the widget factory. Not only is the notion that a leader would try to "manage" the expert scholars and teachers in an academic unit a foreign concept; the cherished precepts of academic freedom and tenure complicate the task of "management"; and the forces of the market, where stars are highly mobile and frequently courted by other institutions, make it difficult indeed to impose rules or constraints. While a certain number of inconvenient and irritating mandates may be accepted as the baseline lot of faculty members, once the hassle factor rises too high, those with options elsewhere may begin to exercise them.

Universities are wonderful, special places: they are filled with smart people doing intriguing work. Taking on a leadership role in one of these vibrant institutions can be an exciting challenge, open up creative vistas, and give you an opportunity to make a difference on a larger canvas than you have before. But to be able to do that, you must be able to recognize and navigate around the danger areas that can turn a dream job into a nightmare. Although smart people can figure out budgetary systems and think clearly about what hiring will strengthen a department, most academics are not prepared for dealing with difficult personnel issues, especially those with legal implications. What do you do if a staff member has a substance abuse problem, if a star faculty member is throwing his weight around or having an affair with a student, if a postdoc accuses a professor of research improprieties, or if it is time to provide an evaluation of a poorly performing employee?

There are always "people problems." Because scholars stepping into leadership roles are often not comfortable with or trained to cope with problems involving conflict or difficult personalities, they do not always address them as effectively as they might. The resulting complications, which can range from strife and dysfunction to litigation, distract from the missions of the institution. These complications can be very costly in financial and human terms, can deplete the pool of talented individuals willing to assume leadership roles, and can take valuable time away from the constructive endeavors of building a high-quality department and improving the faculty, facilities, and future of a program.

For most academics, the people problems are the most difficult aspect of serving in an administrative position. You can work alongside people for years and never learn things about them that becoming a leader may bring (or force) to your attention. Department heads consistently tell me that the hardest part of their jobs is that they learn things about their colleagues they'd rather not know, and then, all too frequently, they have to *talk* about those uncomfortable topics, too. In my two decades as a senior university administrator, I saw a lot of department heads and deans come and go. As far as I can tell, personnel problems are what cause the greatest personal pain and, in consequence, the most resignations from these positions.

It doesn't have to be this way. There are conceptual tools and practical skills that can help academic administrators successfully handle personnel problems, and these skills can be both taught and learned. Acquiring these skills can be the key to having your service as a leader leave a positive legacy. (If you are lucky enough to work in a department that has no outsize egos, disaffected gripers, or simply difficult personalities who distort priorities or make life unpleasant for others, count yourself blessed and use the lessons in this book for giving sage advice to your less fortunate friends and colleagues.)

Although a plethora of books about management have been published—everything from hands-on tricks of the trade to applications of the philosophy of great thinkers to management "systems," from how to use time efficiently to how to run meetings—there is a wide gap between the advice offered in those works and the qualities and challenges specific to academia as it is structured in the United States today. It's hard to apply the usual management rules to special aspects of the academic environment such as lifetime employment security (tenure), a nonhierarchical management structure for key employees, and the self-motivated nature of the creative work involved in research and teaching. This book is intended to fill that gap; its advice is tailored to fit the needs of academic leaders.

Colleges and universities across the country face a leadership gap, as it becomes increasingly difficult to recruit people to serve as department heads and chairs. One reason is surely the lack of support for these thankless yet critical jobs. Department heads are on the front lines of every college and university: in a decentralized organization, they are the face of the university to large numbers of people, and decisions made within departments often determine the quality of the institution's teaching and research programs. Being on the front lines, the heads and chairs are likely targets for the ire of frustrated and disappointed employees, a situation that can be highly stressful. And in our litigious society they are also often targets of lawsuits.

Why do people accept these kinds of positions? To make a positive difference in institutions that are important to our society? For intellectual satisfaction and personal growth? To prevent someone else from taking the job and doing harm to a place and group of people they care about? I'll have more to say later on about the importance of knowing your own reasons. But whatever your reasons, you need to make sure that you don't get consumed by your administrative responsibilities or personally damaged in the process of carrying them out. This book should be useful as you tackle the job. Its purpose is to help you focus on your positive reasons and achieve as many of your goals as possible during your term of service.

For more than twenty years, I served in various offices of the central-campus administration of a major university: in technology transfer, in research administration, in the office of the chief academic officer (the provost), and as a university attorney. I conducted internal investigations into allegations of research misconduct, conflicts of interest, sexual harassment, embezzlement, and more. I became known as the "Department of Yucky Problems," and with a core group of colleagues I introduced new compliance systems, reworked procedures that had violated or otherwise been out of compliance with federal or other regulations, administered and revised a wide range of academic policies, oversaw a grievance system, and worked with the workplace violence prevention team.

Along the way, I noticed patterns and came to recognize common signals of environments going seriously awry. Subsequently I developed a set of programs for providing orientation, training, and support for university administrators, primarily department heads and deans, on the problems academics find the most difficult in their administrative responsibilities—the ones that involve dealing with people. One positive outcome was that, over a period of a decade or more, consistent application of the training and support for front-line administrators resulted in a reduction in the growth of my university's litigation costs related to employment matters. While that wasn't the original goal of our programs to support academic leaders, it was a welcome bonus, especially since fear of being sued is one of the major inhibitors of action by academics who find themselves in difficult situations. I began taking some of these ideas to other universities. Over the years I've worked with thousands of department heads, and those who have adopted the preventive leadership skills I describe in this book report that these ideas and approaches work for them. They can work for you, too.

I come from what I call the train-wreck school of professional ethics. Imagine a train that's just jumped the tracks going around a curve. It's nighttime, so the emergency vehicles are hauling in spotlights and the red lights are spinning. The first steps in responding to an event of this nature always involve removing the injured and stabilizing the wreckage to prevent more damage. Now translate this to the university environment: if the train wreck is an allegation of research misconduct, for example, the first steps, evacuation and stabilization, involve insulating students and others from damage as much as possible and securing the primary data to ensure that a proper investigation can be made. Unfortunately, in universities, the train wreck sometimes induces paralysis and it may take days, weeks, or even months to achieve a consensus that responsive action is necessary. This delay makes the next steps—including a forensic review of what happened to cause the crash—even harder.

After it's acknowledged that a major problem exists, the tracks must be cleared so normal traffic (a.k.a. departmental functions) can resume. After that, it's time to trace the causes of the crash and to examine systems, policies, and procedures to see if they require change in order to prevent future problems. A key question is always whether the crash resulted from one hideous mistake or is part of a pattern. Usually people hope that it was one hideous mistake—preferably by someone they dislike—so that systemic change is not deemed necessary. But it's rare to find an extremely serious problem in a department where good practices have been in effect from beginning to end. It is more likely that the cause of the train wreck was more complex—a combination of bad judgments, crossed signals, poor responses to complaints or warning signs, and a system that didn't work as well as it should have.

It's gratifying to be the one to resolve a serious problem, to be "on the scene" and privy to all the gory details, to figure out how to get the trains moving again. It gets your adrenaline flowing. And it's satisfying to come up with a solution that is as just and even-handed as possible and protects important principles and institutional integrity. It's an ego boost to feel like Solomon. But major problems always cause residual damage to people and/or the institution. You may save the injured and clear away the wreckage, but the crash still happened. Think how much better it would be to have prevented the wreck in the first place. After many years of on-the-scene response and clean-up, I have come to consider preventive efforts far more intellectually challenging and personally satisfying than clean-up efforts. Prevention is less thrilling, but ultimately more creative and subtle work.

Most serious problems can be prevented, and should be. If you approach your job with a clear mind-set and consistently apply a set of concepts and principles to the basics of academic administration, you'll be able to defuse many situations that might otherwise result in personnel losses, grievances, lawsuits, and negative publicity. There's no magic bullet that will make all difficulties disappear, but it's possible to avert large numbers of problems that would otherwise consume disproportionate resources and energy, and to reduce the financial and human costs of the ones that do arise. And, to repeat, the skills to do so can be taught and learned.

To apply preventive management skills and reduce the wear-and-tear factor of people problems requires that you think about your administrative duties as a professional *role*. We all play roles every day. You surely don't behave the same way around everyone in your life. Almost certainly, you have a different persona for dealing with elderly relatives than you do for dealing with your children. You probably have a particular persona that you display in the classroom—and perhaps different ones for introductory undergraduate courses and graduate seminars. And in interactions with peers you undoubtedly present yet another persona. In each persona you are still "you," but different styles are effective in different circumstances. What I'm advising here is that you simply acknowledge and purposefully craft the persona you adopt for your leadership duties.

Think about what it will take to be the "you" who is heading up the department. That "you" may have different attributes in different situations, all rooted in the professional role. Who do you need to be to provide the leadership your unit needs? That's who you need to be to succeed. Has the group been demoralized by a long period of fractured or just plain bad leadership? Does it need a cheerleader? Is the department lacking in resources, so that one of your primary tasks must be to focus on fundraising? Facilities? Stability? Consensus? Challenge? Whatever it is, the purpose of your service as leader is *not* to make you more powerful, attractive, or rich. It's to accomplish institutional goals or advance the institution's overall mission, while also stretching your own horizons.

There are many ways to succeed in these important jobs; your approach must fit your personality and working style as well as the institutional culture. The one nonnegotiable element for success is that you bring a sense of professionalism to the role, an understanding that you are taking on a new relationship to the institution and to your colleagues. You will have to make many difficult choices, especially if budgets are tight. Some people will inevitably be unhappy with one or another aspect of your choices. (Just for the record, there will be some who will be happy, too.)

As teachers and parents know, helping people grow and develop new skills can be among life's most rewarding activities—and can call upon your own talents in new and challenging ways. When you take on a leadership position, you become responsible not only for navigating a course for the group as a whole but also for ensuring that all within your domain have chances to grow professionally. At the same time, you must build for the future of the program, for the individuals in it, and for your own growth, while responding to what will seem, at times, overwhelming demands large and small, important and petty. The approach you take to these challenges, with this book as your guide, can allow you to steer a path that serves the needs of the department, treats people humanely, allows for your personal and professional growth, yet avoids the pitfalls of academic leadership: paralyzing contention, excess stomach acid, sleepless nights, and perhaps lawsuits. It will inoculate you against the worst effects of the people problems by helping you develop tools, perspectives, and a certain immunity to the infections of leadership so that you may use your energies and commitment to leave things better than you found them.

Chapter 1

Embrace Your Fate

It is nearing 6:00 P.M. on your first day as department head. As you are preparing to leave, you receive a drop-in visit from Professor Major, a long-time member of the department with a very high profile in your field. Perching on the corner of your desk, he congratulates you on your new position and commiserates with you about the 20 IQ points you must have lost now that you have become an administrator. He suggests that this is a "great opportunity for us to get a few things straight, so you can be a success in this job."

First, he informs you that, contrary to the published class schedule for next semester, he only teaches on Tuesday afternoon, Wednesday, and Thursday morning, so as to have the weekends free for travel; he is telling you now so you'll have plenty of time to change the course offerings to match his schedule.

Next, he wants you to know that, although he can see why the department has "caved in" to the office staff by no longer requiring them to brew coffee, he finds this acceptable only so long as his office coffeemaker is started by 10 A.M. sharp on his teaching days.

Finally, Professor Major, mentioning that he supported you for the department headship, says he is sure you'll understand that, since he hasn't been assigned a research assistant for the coming year, he will be using his teaching assistant for research tasks, including errands and other routine chores to free him to do his research.

When you take on an administrative role, you become—like it or not—an authority figure. There are few places where this is as problematic as in an academic environment, because ambivalence about authority is pervasive. You've heard the jokes about academic administration being like herding cats, and you've likely made comments yourself about overreaching bureaucrats. Now you've become one. However ambivalent you are about this fate, it is vital to your success that, in a spirit of Nietzschean *amor fati,* you embrace it. Acknowledging your ambivalence, and finding constructive ways to think about it, are important early tasks.

Know Thyself

To survive or even thrive as a leader and manager in an academic setting, you must know yourself. Some focused introspection, in advance, can help prevent overreactions (yours) that might put you at a disadvantage in a charged situation. It can also inoculate you against common ploys of clever manipulators. Not only are these perhaps the most overlooked skills you will need for succeeding, they are also the only ones over which you have total control.

As a starting place, you need to be able to ask yourself, pri-

vately, why you sought or accepted the administrative position—
and come up with real answers. Why are you doing this job? I have
asked thousands of department heads this question in a variety of
settings. The answers invariably boil down to one of four or five:

- To give something back (often initially presented as "It was
  my turn").
- Because I was a better alternative than anyone else (or, less be-
  nignly, "To keep X from doing it and destroying the department").
- To grow in a new dimension (a way to stretch creatively or
  intellectually).
- To make a difference.

I've never had a department head tell me he or she does it for the
money: while the additional stipend can come in handy, money is
not adequate compensation for the burdens of the job—if taken on
conscientiously. It is a major transition to move from a professor-
ship where one largely controls one's own intellectual agenda to a
position in which one can be nibbled to death by administrivia: the
tyranny of the in-box, telephone, drop-in visitors, email, and the
latest form or survey required by some bureaucrat in University
Hall. This other-driven swirl can be overwhelming. To survive and
even thrive in these difficult positions, it pays to know—really
know—why you took on these responsibilities in the first place.

Why did you say yes? Because you thought you could do it
better than others had done it? How? In what dimensions? To leave
the department better than you found it? How, specifically? To
right a wrong? To change the tone? Write down your answer(s).
This is private, so you can burn or shred it as soon as you're done,

but take the time to go through the personal exercise of answering, for yourself, the "why" question.

Once you have a clear understanding of why you agreed to take the job, next take a few moments to articulate two or three (*not more*) goals for your term of service. Formulate specific improvements you would like to make: a global goal such as "making this the best department it can be" is too vague. In what two or three dimensions would you like things to be different (better) when you leave this position than they are now? Is there a way to measure that difference? How will you know if you've succeeded? Force yourself to express your goals in a few simple declarative sentences. It's worth the time to write them down; our brains handle the act of writing differently than simply thinking about something.

Refer back to your goals for your term of service on a regular basis—once a week isn't too often. If you need a written reminder, keep the list in your desk drawer or your wallet. If you're resistant to writing down your goals, say them out loud to yourself at least once. If, after you are immersed in the energy-consuming daily duties and distractions of your job, you keep reminding yourself of these goals, you will be more likely to continue to make progress, however small and incremental, toward their achievement. Without those reminders of why you are doing what you are doing, you can be consumed by activities that may be enervating, depressing, and stressful. With such reminders, you stand a better chance of keeping a sense of your priorities and staying centered.

A caveat: once you know your goals, do not turn them into the academic version of the political stump speech. Unless the goals come out of the environment and are shared by others (such as improving the department's research standing by finding more external funding), you may be seen as excessively careerist to have such goals. It's essential to have these goals for yourself, but proceed cautiously in airing them. They may be different from (but, we hope, complementary to) goals that can be used in discussions with others involved with your unit, from the faculty to the dean to advisory boards or possible donors.

Another important early step is to think about your personal vulnerabilities, and to act, consciously and purposefully, to keep them from diminishing your effectiveness in your new role. What pushes your buttons? What kinds of interactions cause you to overreact? Some people—and they're the ones who will cause you the most misery and stress—have an instinctive ability to find your weaknesses and exploit them. Letting yourself overreact in work settings, responding emotionally or unprofessionally, will put you in the wrong and can shift the focus of the interaction to your conduct instead of the issues. Neither effect is helpful.

You need to know your triggers. If you don't know what sets you off, ask your spouse or your sister. You must also learn to anticipate the triggers and short-circuit or control them so you do not give others power over your reactions. You, and you alone, are in charge of your behavior, and achieving control over your triggers is essential for doing your job. Do not abdicate your self-control to the acts of others. I once worked with a department head (I'll call him Professor Murphy) who was an unusually composed person—unless he felt unfairly blamed, in which case he tended to explode. While his outbursts could be grand theater for observers, they were costly for his effectiveness. Since to others his eruptions seemed almost random, he was seen as not very balanced. Of course, this set up a cycle in which he did get blamed for things, sometimes fairly, sometimes not.

After thinking it through and identifying trigger situations, and after a great deal of trial and error with methods of short-circuiting that were *not* effective for him, Professor Murphy and I contrived a control mechanism that is a bit dramatic but works consistently: when he feels like exploding, he spills something (he's a big coffee drinker), thus disrupting the interaction and buying himself time to regain his self-control. Since he doesn't lose control very often, this approach serves him fairly well. He now has a bit of a reputation for clumsiness, but the occasions on which he loses his composure inappropriately have become almost nonexistent and thus no longer compromise his goals.

The best way to figure out what pushes your buttons, I've found, is to think about interaction patterns in your personal life. Do you have a parent or a sibling who tries to use guilt to get you to do things you don't want to do, and when that happens do you lash out in response, saying things you later regret? Do you have a friend whose chronic lateness or other consistent thoughtlessness accumulates until eventually you overreact? How gracefully do you handle someone's pouting or sulking or otherwise acting out? Do you find yourself avoiding some people after they've disappointed you? If you're uncomfortable with the outcome of a discussion or an interaction, do you go back and raise the same issue over and over?

What is the common element in situations where you say or do things you later wish you hadn't? These are situations in which your buttons are being pushed. Common triggers include feeling blamed, insulted, disregarded, or put down. Unmet expectations— whether or not you ever let others know what they were—can also spark disproportionate reactions. So ask yourself if there is a pattern to the interactions after which you find yourself apologizing or wishing you could rewind and redo.

Perhaps you manage to control yourself when your buttons are pushed, but then find that you can't concentrate, can't sleep, or suffer other symptoms of stress. Do you shut down in certain situations, so that people often worry that you're mad at them? In what situations do you react that way? Those, too, are situations for which you need short-circuiting mechanisms. Life is too short to lose sleep regularly over your work.

Whatever your soft spots may be, think about ways to prevent them from undercutting your effectiveness. Try to develop a strategy for those situations so you are able to behave professionally in the moment, even if you have a different response in private later. You need to learn to stay centered. Instead of losing your temper and snapping at a colleague, the professional response might be to say something like this: "You've raised some good points. I need some time to think about them. I'll get back to you next week." Presenting a consistent, professional persona will be an invaluable asset throughout your term of service. It will help you avoid being manipulated by people who, whether with premeditation or with unconscious skill, provoke reactions to gain the upper hand over you.

Changing your lines can change the script, as the saying goes. This book will give you tools for changing your lines so the script will be less distorted by conflict and personnel problems and the play will have a more predictable and desirable end. You will be more effective and more fulfilled—and you will sleep better, too.

A Professional Home

Beyond knowing yourself, you need to think about your role as an administrator in the institution, the roles of your colleagues, and how those roles interlock. Think about how much of your life is devoted to work: many of us spend more waking hours at our jobs than we do with our families and friends. Your workplace is your professional home, and careful design, good construction, and regular maintenance are required to keep it structurally sound. Let's follow this metaphor for a moment.

The foundation of the entire structure is institutional values. Knowing and being able to articulate the values and principles upon which your professional life rests is your cornerstone. What is your institution's mission? Why does it exist? To whom is it accountable? What constituencies does it serve? If you both know and talk about these matters regularly, you can set a tone that is professional and that will help you make the difficult choices and decisions that will necessarily emerge in your service as a leader. Making choices and decisions rooted in principles and not in personalities will strengthen the foundation of your professional life. If you do not take things personally, it will help others not to do so.

The policies governing academia are the framing—the wood or steel members that rise from the foundation and give shape and form to the structure. In addition to the specific policies of your department and institution, the statements on academic freedom and tenure of the AAUP (American Association of University Professors) are among the framing elements. Are institutional evaluation criteria and procedures implemented as written (brick and steel construction) or not (house of straw)? Are rewards aligned with institutional values and principles, or are the most disruptive members of your department highly rewarded? Whether your compensation packages are published, as is the case in many public institutions, or guarded as institutional "secrets," you may be sure that the relative salary rankings of members of your department will be common knowledge. Everyone will see whose office or lab complex is bigger. The effects on the stability of the structure from alignment (or nonalignment) of rewards with stated values will be pervasive and profound in terms of morale, commitment, or, in contrast, general cynicism.

Two essential elements of the structure of our professional homes that are often taken for granted are expectations for conduct and proper boundaries between the personal and the professional. In our structural metaphor, think of expectations for conduct as the floors and the boundaries between the personal and the professional as the walls that separate our everyday spaces.

Expectations

In academia we do not spend much time communicating the rules for successful conduct. While we provide terms of employment and employee handbooks, these are rarely examined except when a problem arises and someone looks up "the rules" governing that specific situation. Many disciplines have professional ethics statements, but they are not consistently discussed with students and among faculty. Mentoring is spotty, at best, in most institutions. So how and when do our young and emerging professionals receive guidance in the behavior expected to succeed as professionals? If you find yourself frustrated with or disappointed in someone, it may be worth considering whether you've ever let him or her know, in a positive way, what you expect. Have you ever said that you prefer the desks out in the open to be kept reasonably tidy, while the ones in closed offices don't matter so much to you? How do people in your department or group learn which rule applies where? Too often we all run different scripts in our heads, and your expectations may not be met simply because you don't bother to articulate them. As our society and our institutions become increasingly heterogeneous, it becomes ever more important not to assume that "everybody knows" what is expected: mind reading is an imperfect form of communication.

As the leader or authority figure, you have an obligation to set clear expectations for responsible professional conduct and boundaries. It's your job to ensure that the community for which you are serving as steward receives explicit guidance in these areas. To do so, you need to understand what behavior is expected, and then let the members of your department know.

There's a second, harder part of setting expectations: you must also model the desired behavior. Hypocrisy detectors are among our most finely honed human attributes, and "Do as I say, not as I do" is not a successful form of mentoring. To create and maintain a sound professional environment, you will need to think through the messages sent by your words and your conduct. Know yourself in this dimension, too.

Direct supervision of others is difficult, perhaps especially for academics: it feels arbitrary or too personal to say something like "This isn't right," so bad situations tend to persist until they explode. One reason is that saying "It isn't right" can sometimes seem to imply "because I don't like it." It's usually easier to say "The funding agency requires it" or "The dean is making us do this" instead of "I think this is a better way." Here, too, it's important to know yourself. Are you reluctant to state your expectations? If your answer is yes, then you need to overcome that reluctance. Accept the fact that your position entitles, indeed requires, you to set the ground rules and to change what you see needs changing. Take responsibility for the authority you hold by virtue of your position.

Suppose you are overseeing the writing of a grant proposal, and you want every draft to be in the proposal format. You must say what you expect. A student who submits a draft in some other format may have a valid reason, or may not. You won't find out if you don't broach the issue while it's immediate and relatively minor. If you don't make your expectations clear early on, your frustration will increase with each new draft. Your script says the student is incompetent and unresponsive, while the student's script says you're hard to deal with and don't provide feedback or recognition of hard work. If you let your frustration simmer, it may just erupt some day. The target of your ire may (justly) feel unfairly attacked and may be able to adopt victim status or even file a grievance. Others who witness your explosion won't see the long buildup, only your apparently disproportionate reaction. Even if you were right in the first place—months before, by waiting rather than specifying your expectations early on—you will have put yourself in the wrong.

So how do you deal with a perennially tardy secretary? If your department does not have the luxury of an office manager or administrative assistant who supervises the support staff, it may be up to you to deal with this problem. It's a mistake to interpret what's happening through your own lens, concluding that the lateness is evidence of a bad attitude or a lack of commitment to the job before you have enough information. Start with a general, open-ended question: Ask if there's a problem. Perhaps the secretary's tendency to be late stems from a mismatch of daycare starting times, bus schedules, and your office-opening time and doesn't indicate disregard for the work of the office at all. Perhaps the secretary stops to check on an elderly parent every day before work or has a health condition that interferes with her morning routine. Before assuming, ask. If you discover such a problem, explore whether there's any way to adjust the schedule or otherwise address the issues that emerge. But in the first instance, approach the situation in an information-gathering mode before you draw conclusions.

If a solution does not emerge relatively quickly, the next step is to provide a calm and clear statement of expectations: "We need you to be here on time so students who come to our office for assistance don't have to wait and so other staff members don't have to interrupt their own work to cover the desk."

Note how the statement of expectations is tied to the mission and values of the institution. This isn't some personal whim of yours; it relates directly to the secretary's function in the office and in the university. Because people hear and remember conversations differently, and because some people absorb information better through their eyes than through their ears, confirm your conversation in a short note—something like this: "I appreciated the constructive tone of our conversation about your starting time. As I said, it's important that you arrive on time every day so our students can get help when they need it and so others do not have to interrupt their own work to cover your duties. You are expected to open the office by 8:30 A.M. unless you have made advance arrangements, approved by me in writing, to be late."

Confirming your expectations in writing will ensure that both of you will have the same understanding of the conversation. You can't assume that you were clear in the conversation. Your discomfort with being "the supervisor" may have led you to pull your punches or only allude to the problem and your expectations. Putting it in writing afterward (and knowing ahead of time that you are going to do so) is a form of discipline that ensures that you have actually communicated your expectations. The written confirmation also reinforces, in a low-key way, the formality of the situation (this is work, after all) and the relationship between the two of you. Whether you are comfortable with it or not, you are the authority figure, and it is your job to see that the institutional funds spent on the secretary's salary are expended to meet the institutional goals. Finally, in case further action becomes necessary, the note may serve as documentation that you have raised the issue, and at a particular date and time.

Further action is far less likely to be needed if you treat the situation professionally and formally, though not punitively, from the beginning. If, and only if, the problem persists after your early efforts do you start imposing consequences. The consequences you are able to impose will be determined by your institution's policies; be sure you know those policies and are following them when you take this step. There is help to be had in your institution, whether from the personnel office or the legal office—take advantage of this expertise and experience. Each of these consequences should first be communicated orally and then confirmed in writing: "This is the third time in two weeks you have been late. As a result, [specify the consequence]. You are expected to be on time to open the office. If this problem persists, additional action affecting your employment may follow." (In general, good news can be put in writing, but bad news should be delivered in person, even if sensible practice often requires that it then be confirmed in writing.)

You'd be surprised how often this simple (to describe, if not necessarily to do) approach yields the desired results. After all, most people, most of the time, want to succeed. Giving them the information, guidance, and support they need—even when it requires holding a hard conversation—is fairer, and even kinder, than letting problems continue until they're no longer fixable. In addition, it reduces the likelihood of ill-will, complaints, grievances, and even lawsuits—not a trivial point in this day and age. And if such negative developments do occur, a specific, written record of your having provided clear guidance and opportunities to succeed will be of great value in helping to contain the problem.

Before we deal with the complexity of how you're going to respond to Professor Major, let's consider another situation that requires some form of hard conversation.

As the new department head, you have just finished your evaluation of the staff. You call human resources to ask about the possibility of transferring the longtime office manager, Bob Johansen, out of your unit. He is a twenty-two-year employee of the institution, the last seventeen in your department.

You have concluded that Johansen must go for a variety of reasons. He is a disruptive force in the office. He is abrupt and condescending with the staff (a strong and good group of employees, in your assessment), sometimes berating them in a loud voice, and he sometimes refuses to perform certain assigned tasks, citing "previous practice" in the department. You often have to check to be sure he has carried out his responsibilities, and you have been chastised by the college office because reports for which he is responsible have been submitted late and often have been incomplete.

The HR staff member queries you about Johansen's personnel file. You have not previously seen it, but when you retrieve it, you discover two nominations for the campus Professional Excellence Award (copies of which were provided to Johansen), two annual evaluations rating his performance as "superior," and three rating it as "good." There are no other evaluations over his entire time in your department, and no indications of any concern about Johansen's performance, although your associate head tells you that your two immediate predecessors expressed reservations about him. The associate head offers to write down these concerns so you can use them as documentation.

It's clear to you that Bob is a real problem. One reason you took on these administrative responsibilities was to improve the research profile of the department, and one factor in that is the ease (or difficulty) of getting work done. You know the department has a bad reputation in this area, and you think some aspects of it should be simple to fix, but Bob is stubbornly resistant to the changes you want to introduce. Further, you can see that he's causing problems for productive staff members. Moving him out seems like the right thing to do.

Now step back and take a look from a slightly longer perspective. How, specifically, would transferring this staff member affect your goals for the department and your ability to achieve them? What unintended consequences might flow from getting rid of him—for example, what message would that action send about what others in the unit might expect from you? Finally, acknowledge to yourself that your discomfort with doing a hard thing may cause you to be harsher in carrying it out than is healthy for your leadership goals or for Bob Johansen.

Before you make a decision and especially before you start collecting written documentation of events that happened before you arrived on the scene, you must talk to Johansen, and not (at least not yet) for the purpose of firing him. Think of the golden rule: would you feel fairly assessed if you were standing in his shoes? If you had received many official compliments over the years, and yet in your first conversation with your new boss you were dismissed without being given a chance to give your side of the story, let alone a chance to succeed?

Returning to your own shoes, if you're like most people, you do not look forward to meeting with Bob Johansen to discuss this. The dread you're feeling may contribute to a self-fulfilling prophecy. The more you anticipate an unpleasant interaction, the more tense you are likely to be, and your tension increases the likelihood of a confrontation. (If your introspection reveals that this is a type of situation that makes you particularly uncomfortable, it will be worth reflecting on how you can develop and maintain a matter-of-fact and nonpunitive demeanor, so that your behavior in the interaction will be professional and appropriate.)

Moreover, you do not yet have enough information to know whether Johansen needs to go. Jumping directly to that conclusion is unfair and may be mixing your personal feelings with your professional judgments. Maybe you're reacting to information from people you like or have judged as credible without hearing Johansen's side of the story. Maybe you're feeling defensive about criticism from the college office and it's easier to deflect your discomfort by blaming someone else. It's worth disentangling all the threads of your own reactions *and* making sure you have enough accurate information before taking steps that affect someone's job. In other words, you're still at point A or B, and dismissing or transferring an employee should not happen until much later in the alphabet.

Think about Johansen's long-term employment at the university and the department. He has been given written positive feedback, and there is no record of any negative feedback on any aspect of his performance—except the recent complaints from the office staff. Even those are not necessarily reliable information, as, in a *Rashomon*-like way, each of the participants may have different understandings of those interactions. The fundamental question is, has Bob Johansen ever been sent clear messages about how he is expected to contribute to the department's overall mission? From his perspective, he has every reason to believe he *is* contributing: his work has twice been nominated for special recognition.

Your first step, therefore, is to have a conversation with him in which you ask how he thinks things are going and review his current job description. (In fact, it would make sense to have this conversation with every key member of your department.) This is only fair; regardless of whether circumstances have changed and he *can* no longer make a contribution or whether he himself has changed and *is* no longer making a contribution, his perspective is needed. Taking this step sends the message that you're someone who considers all relevant facts before acting; you're informed, judicious, and thoughtful. You are creating a fair and sound structure for others to work within. The key is to ask open-ended questions to which Johansen's responses will give you the longer perspective you need in formulating your decision.

Beyond the fundamental importance of seeking full information before you draw conclusions, you may very well learn important facts that change your view of the situation. Until you talk to Johansen, you know only one version of the story. One of the biggest administrative mistakes you can make is to act on only one version of a story that involves multiple players. Collecting all relevant perspectives will give you a more nuanced understanding and is likely to influence your view of what action is appropriate.

Perhaps you'll learn that Bob is unhappy and would like to change jobs or retire. If that's the case, you won't need to have the hard conversation; you'll be able to bring the situation to a quiet close without any unpleasant confrontation. Few people enjoy doing a bad job; perhaps you'll find out that Bob's duties have drifted since the days when he received commendations for his work, and that he's now being asked to perform tasks he isn't trained for or comfortable doing. In that case, readjusting the distribution of duties among staff members may restore to you a valuable long-term employee without a reduction in your staff (if your institution has imposed a hiring freeze) or without the upheaval of hiring and training a new person. If you haven't done much hiring before, you may not know what a time sink and roll of the dice this can be. Johansen may also have constructive suggestions about how to improve the situation. Alternatively, you may discover that his talents simply cannot be well utilized in your department with its current configuration. Find out what support your university has in human resources and ask someone there for assistance in finding another job at the university that would be a better fit for Bob Johansen; the chances are good that, if he has strong skills, he can go back to being a productive employee when he's no longer a square peg trying to work in a round hole.

Of course, it may turn out that Johansen is oblivious to the problems you see. He may think he's doing just fine and that any problems lie in the changes that have occurred over the years. In that case, you need to don your role as authority figure. But before taking any action, buy yourself some time for reflection: tell him that you will review the distribution of duties and get back to him. For your next interaction with him you'll need the communication skills discussed in the next chapter as well as your clear sense of yourself, your direction, and your goals.

You're still not ready to act on his employment in your unit. It's not time for that—not yet.

Before taking action that affects his job, you must tell him explicitly what you expect of him. You may want to point out that your expectations may be different from those of the previous head. This conversation is not only fair, it is mandatory to protect you legally when you do eventually take action. Since you have already concluded that he needs to go, you may have to adjust your own mind-set before you have additional interactions with him. It is vital that your behavior and your manner be those of an even-handed, objective evaluator, not someone pursuing a personal or discriminatory vendetta.

Because Johansen's personnel file contains only commendations and no recent evaluations, you need to tell him what he is expected to do and how and when he is expected to do it, and to make it clear that he will be evaluated on whether he is meeting those expectations. As a long-term employee, he probably has certain employment rights at the university, and by taking these steps—articulating your expectations for performance and the standards by which he will be evaluated, and then confirming all this in writing, presumably with assistance from human resources—you will be creating documentation that will protect you in the event that he decides to complain or file a grievance about your treatment of him. Expectations should be reasonably specific and stated in positive terms (we'll explore these matters further in Chapter 6). Something like the following would be the first step:

> Dear Bob:
> Let me summarize our recent discussions about your duties
> in the department and the expectations associated with your

position. Consistent with your job description, you are expected to develop the reports required by the college office on time and accurately. Because of recent problems, I am instituting a requirement that you submit drafts of the reports to me two days before they are due. This will give me time to review them and work with you on any needed changes. The drafts you give me should be complete and accurate, and by the third month from now, no further revisions should be necessary at the time of my review. If you are unclear as to the expected format or content, you should seek clarification well before the due date so the reports can be submitted to the college office on time.

You are expected to perform all assigned duties. If you believe that an assignment is not necessary or is contrary to departmental or university policy, you should bring that to my attention, with specific reference to the policy you believe is applicable. My decision as to assignments will be final.

Because it is important that all parts of the office function as a team, you are expected to maintain cordial and professional interactions with all other members of the department. This means that you will give others sufficient time when making requests of them and will provide information sought from you in a timely manner. It is also important that you maintain an appropriate volume when talking to other staff members; please do not raise your voice in conversations.

Cordially,

[your signature]

Evaluations should be directly related to the stated expectations, and should be documented: "Two reports were completed on time and one was not; all reports should be on time in the future or possible employment actions may follow." Bob Johansen should have an opportunity to respond to each evaluation. Again, we will come back to this in later chapters.

Bear in mind that everyone in the unit will be watching the way you handle this and discussing how you and the university treat employees. For you to be able to achieve your other goals, you need them to see you as fair and objective in your treatment of a problem situation; you need their trust and respect. Treating Bob with the dignity befitting his long years of service will serve you and the unit well, even if in the end he leaves the department, voluntarily or otherwise.

You may see this process of providing expectations, performing evaluations, and letting him respond as insufficiently decisive, or as too time-consuming, or as a distraction from meeting your goals for the department or from its "real" business. If, after all these steps, the outcome is that he must go, you may feel frustrated by the slow pace of change. But proceeding in a deliberate way that provides opportunities for him to succeed will serve you and the unit better in the long run. Precipitous action might have unintended consequences, from loss of trust to a grievance or even a lawsuit charging you with discrimination. Don't be like the administrator whose term wasn't renewed, despite his having achieved many good changes, because he had caused so much disruption and uncertainty in the unit that the consensus was that he left "too much roadkill" in his wake.

Taking this slowly, and giving Bob Johansen a genuine opportunity to remedy the shortcomings in his job performance, is more likely to serve your goal of making things better in the department by the end of your term of service. It's to your advantage to help him succeed, either in his current position or elsewhere. If you can salvage a good, experienced employee, all the better. Even if that doesn't happen and he departs, others in the unit will have seen you working through this problem deliberately and fairly. Both by earning their trust and by setting a good example for their own behavior, you will have strengthened the professional environment in your department. Keeping this desirable outcome in mind can help you get past your discomfort with becoming an authority figure and temper your craving for instant results.

Giving the person under review a chance to bring his or her conduct in line with your expectations is not only fairer to that person, it is fairer to others in the environment who are doing their jobs with care and professionalism. It is a far better way of proceeding than either firing the person abruptly or allowing the problem to persist without intervening. After all, what message would you be sending to the conscientious members of your department if you did not address, or even acknowledge, an employee's out-of-bounds conduct because you were so deep into an avoidance strategy?

The method I have outlined works for problem groups as well as individuals, though with groups you'll need an approach that acknowledges preexisting group standards and habits. You need to establish expectations through some advance work of your own. The first step is to reflect about what characteristics are already present in the unit that you want to reinforce. If your unit generally resolves disputes without personal attacks, for example, work on reinforcing this positive characteristic. The next time a problem is solved in a faculty meeting, you might say something like this: "I've always been pleased to be associated with this department because one of our hallmark traits is that we focus on problems, not personalities."

This approach also gives you a way to deal with department members whose actions do not conform to the group's ethos. Thus, if someone resorts to personal criticism of a colleague, you can say, with a sincere tone and a straight face: "One great thing about this department is that we discuss problems without getting personal. I'm very interested in your comments, so will you please rephrase them so we can focus on your suggestion?" Having laid the foundation earlier by putting this idea into circulation, you will probably see nodding heads around the room when you speak. This nonverbal expression of the group values can be surprisingly powerful in moderating undesirable behavior, even in your department's most difficult members. We will return to this idea later. For now, think about the importance of individual and group expectations in maintaining the soundness of a professional environment and relate them, where you can, to the concept of boundaries between personal and professional conduct.

Boundaries

I often turn to the idea of Janus, the ancient Roman god of doorways and gates, when thinking about boundaries. In his role as guardian of doorways, Janus guards boundaries, both physical and temporal, so that he is also the god of new beginnings. Because most issues of ethical conduct require a clear awareness and understanding of appropriate behavioral boundaries, oversight by such a god is just what many professionals need. May the god of boundaries bless your leadership.

Even though you (in the course of knowing yourself) have internalized/learned the importance of boundaries between personal and professional roles, who provides this lesson to faculty members? Where do faculty members, especially new assistant professors, receive guidance on setting appropriate boundaries between their personal lives (which may be close to nonexistent in some disciplines, given time-consuming professional demands) and their professional lives? When we give people authority over others who are not very different from them in age and life situation—teaching assistants over undergraduates and assistant professors over graduate students, for example—do we give them guidance about sound professional boundaries? What messages are sent and received about such boundaries if, for example, senior faculty are allowed to make students run personal errands for them, or, more commonly, to require consistently unreasonable hours in the lab?

It's a truism that everyone in universities feels powerless: undergraduates are at the mercy of everyone, their teaching assistants (who rarely recognize their power over their students and thus can be ripe for abusing it) feel they are at the bottom of the power curve, assistant professors feel disenfranchised and powerless, associate professors worry about those who can vote on their promotion, full professors must jockey for position and perks, and department heads *know* they have very little real power. But power there is, both real and perceived, in all these situations. Pretending it isn't there doesn't make it go away.

Not only must you understand the difference between exercising institutionally conferred power for personal and professional ends, but everyone in your unit must have the same understanding. Thus a teaching assistant should comprehend that it is an abuse of her power over her undergraduate students to offer extra credit to anyone who lends her a suitcase for her job interviews, regardless of how easygoing the classroom atmosphere may be. An assistant professor should grasp how difficult candor can be for a graduate student who is asked "Are you available to babysit for us this Saturday?" A person with supervisory responsibilities—and especially evaluations that affect salary determinations—should be clear about the lines between official duties and personal favors like running out to get coffee or a birthday card for a spouse. No matter how friendly the office relationships, having a staff member pick up your kids after school so you can go to an important meeting is a blurring of personal and professional boundaries, especially if done on the university time clock. It's true that private universities have more leeway than public ones in terms of what falls within the scope of employment, but personal services and personal interactions are complicated when there are supervisory relationships, whether those are educational or based on employment.

The decentralized and generally informal, even antiauthoritarian, nature of academia tends to send mixed messages about these boundaries, a situation that makes a keen awareness of and respect for them even more crucial than in other workplaces. As well, the large quantities of public money and trust invested in universities—public and private alike—mean that there are additional responsibilities and constituencies beyond the ones that may first come to mind. All these complexities mean that the clarity provided by crisp boundaries is beneficial.

Good boundaries are needed to separate personal interactions from professional decisions. Think about how much harder it is to be fair to people you don't like than to those you do. One of the most successful department heads I have worked with told me that, while he personally liked some members of his department and didn't like others at all, his goal was that no one ever be able to tell which was which by the way he dealt with them. My observation of the department led me to conclude that he was meeting that goal. The consistency of the cordial courtesy with which he treated each and every member of the unit provided him with a valuable base from which to make significant changes in the culture of the department. It is harder than you might imagine to achieve this effect, but it's worth striving for. If you keep an eye on why you have taken on this leadership role and what you stand for in the role, it will help you maintain those boundaries, which will contribute to the overall health of your unit.

And Now for Professor Major

The deliberate, step-by-step approach to the Bob Johansen problem allows you to fulfill your responsibilities to the people in your unit, to the department, and to the university, not to mention keeping yourself out of grievances and lawsuits. But it doesn't arm you for dealing with Professor Major's drop in visit. Your colleague used a number of potent maneuvers on you, from mixing personal and professional topics to implicitly threatening your success and playing on your desire to do well in your new role.

First, by coming in after regular working hours as you're preparing to leave, Major picked a time when a degree of informality would attach to the situation. The hours after 5 P.M., especially in administrative offices, are usually a quiet time, when the telephones don't ring, the email slows down, and conversations tend to be more relaxed than during regular business hours. Unless you have let it be known that you enjoy talking with people after five, to arrive so late—and especially to drop by unexpectedly—is to assert a personal connection to you.

Professor Major's opening conversational gambits carry an undercurrent designed to make you uncomfortable: you've lost status by becoming an administrator, and he's in a position to help ensure your success if you follow his guidance. The three items he raises with you—his teaching schedule, the coffee, and his intentions for his teaching assistant—reinforce his power play. What they have in common is the point that the rules that apply to others in the department do not apply to him. He's special, and he expects you to grant him special privileges in recognition of his status.

Even without the power-play elements, the desire among academics for special treatment in recognition of their particular qualities and/or status is a theme that will recur throughout your tenure as an administrator in higher education. Academia is filled with insecure overachievers who—no matter how high their objective level of achievement or recognition—fear that they're not worthy of their success and that at any moment they may be exposed as frauds (this phenomenon, which can be found both inside and outside academia, has come to be known as "imposter syndrome"). Getting you to confirm their value by granting them special treatment is thus a driving need, and one that you cannot simply ignore or dismiss. If you've ever been puzzled by someone's insistence on what seemed to you a trivial change or requirement, it may make more sense if you interpret it in this light. If you can learn to recognize this pattern—which is omnipresent—and find effective ways to deal with it, you will have a secret weapon in your efforts to leave things better than you found them.

Implicit in all of this is that you have become an authority figure, one whose opinion matters. Many find this a difficult concept to internalize—it's not just your own peculiar barrier. But to succeed in your new role, you must come to terms with the nature and limits of your authority and become comfortable with it, so you can exercise it with grace and finesse. So: How do you meet the needs of those who are key to your unit's success while also maintaining an ethical climate, making principled decisions, and treating everyone fairly? What do you do about Professor Major?

Articulate the Issues

First, you need to be able to articulate to yourself what's going on in a given situation. Stop and think about the central interaction. What's the tone of the encounter? What are the signals sent by the location, time, jokes, body language, and requests? By arriving at an hour when your workday was supposedly over, Major invaded your private time. By perching on your desk, he invaded your personal working space. He twice mentioned that he supported you for the position. It's not unreasonable to see his behavior as a power play with an implied threat to your success in the job if you don't keep him happy.

The three items he lists as necessary to keep him happy are all likely to cause you concern. Let's examine his requests from various perspectives. Who are the stakeholders, the people who may be affected by any decisions you make? What policies apply to each of his requests? What precedents exist or may be set by your decisions? And how quickly do you have to decide?

Stakeholders

Stakeholders are people who will be (or will think they are) affected by a given decision. They are the ones who, if they complain about the action you take, will be given a respectful hearing.

The people affected by the teaching schedule are students, instructional staff, and the support staff who prepared and disseminated the schedule and would have to do that work again if you revised it. There are issues of equitable division of labor in the department as well as access to desirable times and rooms. Presumably your unit has some set process by which faculty members indicate their preferences for which courses they teach and when. If this process was followed, those involved in administering it may have a stake in your response as well.

In the coffee matter, the group most affected by your decision will be the staff members who used to make the coffee and who may be reassigned to do so. But, assuming that your predecessor's decision to relieve them of that task was made carefully and after consultation, your ruling about the coffee will send the entire department a message about your willingness to stick to well-considered policies. (Note the assumption that decisions were made carefully; if you believe or find that they were not, then treating them with respect may not be a good step. But let's assume for now that those who came before you had sound reasons for their actions.)

As for Major's third request, the duties assigned to a teaching assistant concern all faculty and teaching assistants in the department, and possibly outside the department as well. If your campus has unionized assistants, there will also be a legal dimension. Issues of equity, boundaries, and educational goals are implicated in the potential use of the teaching assistant for "routine chores" to free Major to do his research. Why are students on your campus appointed as teaching assistants? Are there delineated duties for them in a campus policy manual or handbook? Do teaching assistants receive any academic credit for their service? In many ways, this element of the problem with which Professor Major has presented you is the most complex and likely to impinge on the largest number of stakeholders.

Once you have identified the stakeholders, it's a good idea to think about either consulting them as part of the decisionmaking process and/or informing them of your decision before it becomes public. You can't please everyone in the department all of the time, but you may be able to soothe (or prevent) some people's ruffled feelings by soliciting input before you make the decision or by telling them personally about the decision and your reasoning instead of letting them hear about it through the grapevine or in an impersonal announcement.

Policies and Procedures

What university or department policies govern the decisions you're about to make? You need to know what these policies are. Ask yourself (or better yet, a knowledgeable secretary or administrative assistant) what policies your department, college, or university has on any of these matters. If you know or are told of policies, are they written down? Do you know where they are? If you agree to any of Professor Major's requests, will you be applying or changing an overall policy or making an exception to a general rule? Can you articulate the basis for your decision?

Another way to think about this dimension is to ask yourself which aspects of each issue are under your personal control. Is there a procedure you should follow to come to a decision, or will it be enough to decide as you think best? One benefit of relying upon policies and procedures (especially written ones) for reaching outcomes is that it depersonalizes the decisions. Since Major has made such a strenuous effort to personalize your conversation and to put you on the spot, every tool that will reduce that aspect of the interaction will help you. Both invoking the roles and rights of other stakeholders and applying relevant policies may be to your advantage.

For example, Major's plan to require his teaching assistant to run

errands and help with his research may raise not only issues of equity within the department but also legal or contractual problems.
Students might file grievances, and the institution's rules on ap-
pointments and compensation might be violated. If teaching assistants are paid on a different scale from research assistants, legal issues
could intrude. If your assistants are unionized, the situation could
be even dicier.

This may sound grim, but actually it can be very good news. To
be constrained by policies, to have your hands tied, can be a great
advantage. No matter how reluctant Major may be to recognize
that there are larger issues involved than his individual preferences,
you may be able to defuse his animosity against you by reframing
the issues to make the contracts and policies the bad guys. Focusing
his ire on their deficiencies may take some of the heat off you. (Of
course, this isn't guaranteed to work. If he is fixated on having a research assistant but doesn't qualify by your institution's standards, he
may have enough ire to encompass both the policies and you.)

If Professor Major qualifies for a research assistant under departmental policies, or if you can find—or help him find—resources
for one, he may be mollified for the moment. Here's where one of
the main counterintuitive aspects of your new line of work may
first rear its head. Even if you manage to satisfy his request, albeit
not in the form originally presented, he may still be critical of you
and speak ill of the way you handled the situation. This will be your
first taste, if it occurs, of situations in which the interaction is not
about the topic presented, but about some other sort of need altogether, one that you may never succeed in meeting. I'll say more
about that particular dilemma later in this book.

But let's posit the more probable outcome, which is that you are
unable to give Professor Major what he wants. Even if your efforts

to shift the responsibility to the policy fail and he blames you personally, you'll be on stronger ground when he starts complaining
about you if you've framed all the issues in terms of the university's
policies.

Precedents

Before acting on any of Professor Major's requests, stop and think
about the likely ripple effects of each of your impending actions. If
you give him what he wants, who else will want the same deal?
Who will want previous decisions modified? Can you live with the
consequences of extending a particular privilege to others? How
easily will you be able to deny such requests? How unpleasant will
that be?

Certainly, for example, agreeing to change the class schedule to
fit Major's preference—especially if his wishes were known and
considered before the schedule was set—will stimulate many other
faculty members to ask for similar concessions. Here's a useful exercise. Suppose you allow Major to set his own teaching schedule, but
you are likely to refuse to grant others the same privilege: what
words will you use to turn them down? Try saying those words out
loud, imagining that you're denying Professor Minor's request for
exactly the same special treatment Professor Major is seeking. Do
they sound convincing?

In that light, think about what will happen when your decision
becomes public. How will others react to it? Will they understand
and respect it, and thus respect you? What version of the story will
the grapevine be likely to carry? Major has the new department
head under his thumb? The new head can't stand up to a temper
tantrum? Or the head is willing to listen to reasonable arguments?
What message do you want to convey as you start your term of ser-

vice? Because there will be one. You may not get to choose it, but your actions will definitely influence its content.

Timing

How quickly must you make the decisions? For a variety of reasons, you may not want to accede to any or all of Major's demands. But he is likely to apply a good deal of pressure to secure what he wants, and to get it sooner rather than later. What can you do?

You need time to think the situation through and figure out what policy, procedure, or principle applies to each issue. So above all, buy time.

End the conversation by pleading another obligation—and then start packing up to leave. Offer Major an appointment to discuss the issues later. When my oldest daughter was small, she coined a term that always comes to my mind under such circumstances. When asked to do something she didn't want to do, she would hold up her hand and solemnly inform me: "Mommy, I'll do that another later." What you seek now is to defer this whole discussion to "another later." Whatever it takes, avoid making any commitments on the spot. Plead fatigue. Mention others who need to be consulted. If the professor accuses you of being indecisive, agree. Just don't make any promises. If desperate, try turning the conversation and asking Major about his latest intellectual coup or his travel plans to get him talking about himself. But make and hold the boundary that you're not going to give an answer on the spot.

Finally, when your briefcase is packed, leave your office. Turn out the light. Lock the door. Go to your car. You need some time to think, and to consult. Tomorrow is another day, in the well-known words of Scarlett O'Hara. Tomorrow will be soon enough for you to begin consulting with the central stakeholders, building coalitions to support the outcomes the consultations suggest, and preparing to inform Professor Major of your decisions.

If you can do just this—delaying any substantive response to Major's demands to give you time to consider them, and foiling his power play by scheduling the continuation of the discussion at a time of your own choosing—you will have made your first steps toward a successful tenure. You will be on the road to knowing and using your professional persona as a leader.

Chapter 2

Know Your Colleagues

Y ou are the chair of a fifteen-member department, and in the past week three faculty members have come to tell you about their conversations with the same graduate student, Sally Smithson.

Ms. Smithson has confided in each of them that she has ended a consensual involvement with an untenured faculty member, Dr. Thomas Foster, but that she feels pressure from him to resume the relationship. His unrelenting pursuit has become frightening, including visits and telephone calls in the middle of the night. Dr. Foster is on her thesis committee, and according to her, he has suggested that if she doesn't go back to him, her thesis is likely to require a great deal of additional work. She takes this as a threat. She has pledged the faculty members to secrecy, but each is disturbed enough about the situation to consult privately with you. They tell you that she has also consulted with the Office of Women's Programs and with the Ombudsperson.

Foster is up for tenure this year. Ms. Smithson does not want to file a formal complaint for fear that complaining would hurt her career. And yet, at the same time, she doesn't think he ought to get tenure, and she hopes her revelations will affect that decision. She wants those with whom she has consulted to help her extricate herself from the situation while also maintaining her confidentiality.

A highly talented administrator once told me, in a moment of frustration: "In my next job, there'll be no personnel." A large majority of the most difficult problems are caused by a small fraction of the people in any environment: you'll spend far more time dealing with them than you ever imagined or wanted. Friction inevitably arises when people work together, and the academic environment has some special aspects that can complicate an already fraught set of problems. These include the star system, academic freedom, the general reluctance of those in academia to be managed, and disdain for those in management positions. Professor Major, for example, is a star who likes to throw his weight around.

Presumably, one of your goals in accepting this job is to improve your department or your college. By instituting good practices like the habit of creating and maintaining sound professional boundaries, by affirming positive group qualities, and by managing for the good of the whole, you will make large strides toward your goal. Consider how the habit of maintaining boundaries and common pacts about confidentiality would have helped in the situation with Sally Smithson. Dr. Foster violated an important boundary by becoming personally involved with a student under his supervision. The three other faculty members violated pledges of confidence to a student—pledges they should not have made in the first place. And in doing so they dropped the original problem, compounded by the breach of confidentiality, in your lap.

The tendency of people to "delegate upward" by passing problems along—moving the burden (or the monkey) from their own backs to those of their managers—has been described in a well-known article published in the *Harvard Business Review*, "Managing Management Time: Who's Got the Monkey?" While a university is not a business, no matter how extensively presidents and trustees import "businesslike" practices, this tendency operates in academia as well. In the scenario sketched above, the three faculty members transferred the "monkey" to you, their department chair, when they betrayed Smithson's confidence. Instead of telling Smithson that they felt obliged to consult with you, they promised her secrecy without knowing enough about the circumstances to know whether the pledge could be kept. Then they all violated the promise by reporting to you, leaving that monkey on your back. (In fact, situations like this—allegations of sexual harassment—fall into a highly regulated area, and the faculty members probably *cannot* keep the confidence under applicable legal policies and standards. We'll look more at such items in Chapter 6.) Clear thinking about personal versus professional obligations and appropriate confessional boundaries is a good habit that can be learned by conscious discussion and practice. Its absence here in the faculty members makes an already difficult situation worse.

Impediments to Good Practice

Some specific features of academia make implementing good practices tricky. First and foremost, the environment is very decentralized: a college or university comprises a multitude of microclimates, some of which resemble feudal fiefdoms. From the culture within a particular laboratory to that in a group of offices physically isolated from the rest of the department, you'll find that you have to engage with multiple cultures and climates. This segmentation contributes to the development of situations like the one between Foster and Smithson, because so much that happens in an academic environment happens out of the sight of others.

As if that isn't enough of a challenge, these microclimates have a significant temporal quality: they have some people who have been there "forever" (for decades) and others who stay only a few years. There is a huge annual turnover in the community's population. The long-timers may resist change (they've waited out previous department chairs and their new ideas, so they can wait you out, too). Meanwhile, because multitudes of students come and go, a major effort at communication this year may need to be repeated next year and the year after that to have any meaning for the newcomers—but may be boring to those who have heard it all before.

To top it off, while you're trying to communicate goals, aspirations, good habits, and positive expectations, you'll also be expected to "educate all members of your department" about the latest rules promulgated by the central administration, from how to fill out the new time- and activity-report forms to the Office of Occupational Safety's new procedures for recycling transparencies. And this is all taking place in an environment with inconsistent internal communication systems and poorly developed habits of interaction. Unless you're very lucky and have acquired your responsibilities in a unit with a tradition of warm collegiality and frequent interchange among its members, it's likely that some members of your unit do not routinely interact with others. This lack of connection may be by design or oversight, but if this exists to any significant degree, it may complicate your efforts. Email can help with communicating new rules about recycling, but is unlikely to be an effective way to change ingrained patterns of behavior.

Other features of the academic environment will also complicate your new job. Some of those features are academic freedom and tenure, the concept of collegiality, the academic star system, and the perennial problem of scarce resources.

Academic Freedom and Tenure

Contrary to what many people think, academic freedom does not provide a license for any and all classroom utterances, nor does it license academics to neglect duties or to abuse students or colleagues. The foundation documents defining academic freedom can be found in the "Redbook" of the American Association of University Professors (AAUP). Central to those documents is the concept that both privileges and responsibilities are conferred upon professors by their membership in the "community of scholars." The critical freedom to pursue scholarship, even about unpopular ideas, is accompanied by certain responsibilities: to "be accurate," to "exercise appropriate restraint," and to "show respect for the opinions of others."

> Think of the problem of Professor Strasse. You've heard that
> he has been projecting images of classic paintings by Rubens,
> many featuring nude women, in his calculus class, and that he
> refers to students who object to these visual presentations as
> "cretins" and "assholes." Your last conversation with him on
> this topic was not very successful, in your view. When you

told him you'd been getting complaints from students and parents that the pictures were offensive or irrelevant, he dismissed the objections as evidence of narrow, provincial attitudes, claimed that the paintings were part of his teaching method, and reminded you that academic freedom gives him the absolute right to speak as he pleases in his teaching.

Yet if you review the Redbook you will know that Professor Strasse's claim of the right to speak as he pleases in his teaching is a misinterpretation of the concept of academic freedom. His pejorative characterizations of his students are not exercises of academic freedom, because that freedom does not extend to speaking to students in that way. He may be held accountable and even reprimanded for such conduct without any infringement upon his academic freedom. Note, however, that you're not home free: the insults that violate the requirements to "exercise appropriate restraint," and to "show respect for the opinions of others" are unfortunately likely to fall in a different category from the images he projects in the classroom, especially in light of his claim that the images are related to his pedagogy. The problem of how to deal with Professor Strasse is really two different problems, and only the name-calling may straightforwardly be addressed with sanctions of some sort if he does not alter the behavior. You may find, though, that if you can successfully address one bad habit by invoking professional norms, it may become easier to deal with other troubling aspects of the professor's conduct.

Like academic freedom, tenure is a feature of academic life that, although it shields its holders in certain ways, does not give them carte blanche to behave as they please. You may well hear, when you seek support to address Strasse's habit of insulting students,

"He's got tenure, so there's nothing we can do about it." According to the Redbook, the tenure system is designed to ensure unfettered scholarly inquiry—"freedom of teaching and research and of extramural activities"—and to give professors a degree of financial security. Here are the key sections of the statement:

> Institutions of higher education are conducted for the common good and not to further the interest of either the individual teacher or the institution as a whole. The common good depends upon the free search for truth and its free exposition.
>
> Academic freedom is essential to these purposes and applies to both teaching and research. Freedom in research is fundamental to the advancement of truth. Academic freedom in its teaching aspect is fundamental for the protection of the rights of the teacher in teaching and of the student to freedom in learning. It carries with it duties correlative with rights.
>
> Teachers are entitled to freedom in the classroom in discussing their subject, but they should be careful not to introduce into their teaching controversial matter which has no relation to their subject. Limitations of academic freedom because of religious or other aims of the institution should be clearly stated in writing at the time of the appointment.
>
> College and university teachers are citizens, members of a learned profession, and officers of an educational institution. When they speak or write as citizens, they should be free from institutional censorship or discipline, but their special position in the community imposes special obligations. As scholars and educational officers, they should remember that the public may judge their profession and their institution by their utterances. Hence they should at all times be accurate, should exer-

cise appropriate restraint, should show respect for the opinions of others, and should make every effort to indicate that they are not speaking for the institution.

Tenure gives faculty members procedural protection against arbitrary institutional action—but it does not and cannot protect those who abuse their positions. Thus to throw up one's hands and accept bad conduct on the grounds that tenure makes any other action impossible is a cop-out.

Collegiality

We have seen that neither Professor Strasse's denigration of his students nor Dr. Foster's (alleged) sexual involvement with a student would be an exercise of academic freedom. However, this is not the only objection you may encounter to the idea of taking action against faculty members' bad behavior—or even to just gathering facts in such a situation. The concept of collegiality is strong in academia, and it is misunderstood at least as often as—maybe more often than—academic freedom or tenure.

Once, years ago, I was asked to deal with a letter that arrived while the university provost I worked for was out of town. In two typed pages, the head of a university department reported that a faculty member had threatened to kill him, and asked for the provost's protection. I called the department head and suggested that there were people in the university whose job was to protect other people—and that the word did begin with *P*, but that it wasn't *provost*, it was *police*. He responded: "Do you know how uncollegial it would be for me to call the police on my colleague?" I asked him how collegial it had been for his colleague to threaten to kill him.

It is not atypical, in universities today, to feel that taking on problems rooted in personal conduct might not be "collegial." I've been
told at one time or another that it wouldn't be collegial to discuss
safety concerns raised by the apparent drinking problem of a faculty member who taught in a lab with high-pressure equipment
because drinking was an issue of "personal conduct." And that it
would violate collegiality to ask a highly regarded research associate
to stop talking about his interest in women's underwear with the
department secretaries. I've also heard respected academics express
grave concern about the propriety of reviewing a colleague's work
in the face of significant evidence of shoddy (at best) or fraudulent
(at worst) data, on the grounds that "it's simply not collegial to sit
in judgment of a colleague" or "we don't do witch hunts here."
(Many of these individuals are at the same time avid supporters of
the proposition that funding agencies should provide research support only on the basis of peer review.)

Collegiality does not mean tolerating any and all conduct in a
professional setting. It does not stipulate or support ignoring bad
conduct, especially behavior that is detrimental to the health, safety,
or productivity of others in the environment. So if your colleagues
urge you to overlook students' complaints about Professor Strasse's
verbal style because addressing it wouldn't be "collegial," you need
to think through and have a firm understanding (one that you can
communicate) about what collegiality encompasses and what it
does not.

Many damaging actions are defended—improperly—under the
guise of "collegiality." Collegiality matters in the community of
scholars. The academic enterprise depends upon trust and the robust exchange of ideas. The protocols that have evolved to protect
those values must not be twisted so that they shield abusive or ex-

ploitative conduct. The community has a right to function, and each of its members must contribute to that functioning through an educated awareness of what does and does not support those values. It is your role, as authority figure, to ensure that members of your department do have such an awareness.

Academic Stars

The star system is alive and well in American universities. The recruitment of a big name can help put a university on the map, bring in significant funding for research, or at least make a media splash and impress donors. Such stars are much sought after by other institutions, and retaining them can be a challenge. Those a tier down from true supernovae (and sometimes even the comets and meteors who are burning out) can also command considerable attention and resources. And if these people are among the insecure overachievers I mentioned in Chapter 1, their need for reassurance will frequently prompt them to seek special privileges befitting their "special" status.

Have you encountered the faculty member who insists on meeting with the provost or the president on a semi-regular basis to describe his latest projects and give advice about university governance? Usually he seeks the first meeting by suggesting that, owing to the inability of his department head or dean to understand him (and his value to the institution), he will have to begin considering outside offers, albeit with a heavy heart due to his allegiance to the institution. After that first meeting, unless the provost or president has good boundaries and great personal charm, future meetings will be necessary "unless you don't find my modest suggestions to be of any help." This form of emotional blackmail is often successful and rarely seen for what it is or the way it can distort policies, procedures, and the institutional decisionmaking structure.

Of course, such meetings may cost nothing but time, and being courteous and respectful toward valuable intellectual assets is only common sense. The rub comes in what topics are discussed, and whether these little chats come to supplant meaningful departmental or college oversight of the faculty member. All too often the faculty star manages to make the provost or the president the only person in the institution to whom he has to report, and to consider himself accountable to no one else.

If you have a star in your unit who does not seek such reassurances or special treatment, stop reading right now and review what you've done recently to express your appreciation—don't get complacent and forget to count your blessings. If you haven't rewarded this humble creature lately, find something nice you can do for him or her and do it immediately. Far more numerous are the other sort, to whom you must constantly respond or about whom you must constantly worry as they solicit external offers to improve their lot in the university.

An aside: If you're constantly caught in the escalation game— asked to match the level of salary or perks in outside offers—it might be worth thinking about whether your institutional policy is clear enough about how often this game can be played. Your star (and others) will still receive the offers and play the game, but you may be able to reduce the frequency if there's a rule, especially if it comes from one or two layers above you. Chances are, it will benefit the entire institution to have a clearly expressed (and followed) rule about how often offers are met. In terms of preventive management and good institutional habits, reflect upon how faculty members will spend their time if the only way to get a significant raise is to receive an outside offer. Does such a system create an incentive to concentrate upon teaching, research, and service? Of course not: if the reward structure is built around external offers, even a smart person—one, for example, with a Ph.D. from a major research university—can figure out that a way to get the highest return on time spent is to solicit job offers.

If you sense that your star seeks special treatment for the sole purpose of gauging your esteem (today), it's worth trying to cultivate a mind-set of putting any privileges you consider granting into a context of the institution's values. That is, think about how you could frame whatever you are giving your star so that anyone else in the department who reaches the same level of achievement will receive the same treatment. A good example of this is the policy at Berkeley that every faculty member who wins a Nobel Prize receives a personalized parking space (reserved, with his or her name on the sign).

Inevitably, you will sometimes have to make compromises to propitiate a star. When this happens, try to align these compromises with institutional values, and to express them in a way that, as much as possible, levels the playing field for all future stars. What perquisite offered by your institution might be analogous to Berkeley's reserved parking spaces? Try to link the privilege or reward granted the star to a documented achievement: recognition by a professional society, publication of a tenth book, etcetera. Framing the reward this way—Star A got Special Treatment B because of Achievement C—will reduce jealousy, even among those who do not and will never achieve at that level, because the concept that the granting of the privilege is aligned with the values of the institution will help mitigate resentment. Of course, you'll have to be prepared to provide Special Treatment B to anyone who delivers

Achievement C, so choose your framing device carefully. Don't run out of parking spaces.

Professor Strasse, in the situation described earlier in this chapter, is claiming special status that is neither protected by academic freedom nor aligned in any way with the institution's best interests. To reward his behavior by ignoring it to the detriment of the students in his classes is the opposite of this advice to seek to align special treatment, where necessary, with the value system of your institution.

Do your best to cultivate appreciation among all members of the department of the benefits that the achievements of one member confer on the whole. Stars can shed light: celebrate accomplishment and frame it as good for everyone. One of the most corrosive things that can happen to a department is when its most successful members and those who are most beneficial to the department and the institution are resented by their colleagues. This can happen even if they are not personalities who demand special treatment (though it tends to be more common in those circumstances).

A group with a predominance (or even just a critical mass polluting the rest) of members who resent the best among them is destined for a rough time, with a likelihood of a downward trend in quality: if it becomes known (or even just suspected) in your field that high achievers have difficult daily lives in your department because of the resentment of others (especially lower achievers), potential stars will be less eager to join your faculty. Thus framing the accomplishments of the stars in terms of the benefits they bring the unit as a whole is both good for the stars (as it acknowledges and articulates their importance to the institution) and good for the atmosphere and functioning of the department. Do this carefully, so you are not just adding to the star's leverage for the next round of demands. If you do it well, you'll encourage the star to take pride (bask, even) in benefiting the department, and you'll establish a foundation from which to argue, when faced with later requests, that a form of special treatment that might be detrimental to the unit is not in the star's interests either.

As an example, suppose that Professor Stellar attracts more top-quality students than she can handle alone. You'd welcome the influx of so much talent into the department, but you don't want students to arrive with unrealistic hopes of working with Stellar and then become disappointed and disgruntled. In this situation, it pays to think hard about how you can structure the student experience so that the star can still serve as a draw but can also divert some of the applicants to other faculty members. This is a nontrivial issue, which requires both management of perceptions and adroit logistical sleight-of hand. Strategize carefully and lay groundwork well in advance of launching such an endeavor. It can be a high-risk, but also a high-payoff, venture.

Elements to manage include the star's thinking, the faculty's perceptions, and the actual experience of the students. Let's consider the last item first. You want the students to feel that in your department they receive an exemplary welcome and a first-class education with a good placement after graduation—plus access of some sort to Professor Stellar. If you can pull that off, everyone can emerge a winner. Stellar will feel important for attracting students and magnanimous for being a good citizen of the unit, other faculty and the overall unit will reap myriad benefits from the presence of talented students, and the students will be pleased with their experience. As the department's reputation for having good students rises, it will attract even more good students, its ratings are likely to improve, and so on.

Of course, if Professor Stellar lords it over others, or if other faculty members treat the students as Stellar's cast-offs, the situation may be detrimental to quality. To avoid such a negative outcome, you need to prepare in advance to manage the department's perception of whose idea the whole experiment is (hint: not yours), and to package the proposal carefully for each of the participants.

For Stellar, you want to package the proposal as a chance for her to help the department: she can be the rising tide lifting all boats. The packaging will also have to deal with the fact that for this good deed she won't receive individual acclamation. You may want to work on subtle ways to convey the idea that the truly superior intellect is so secure that it does not require public acknowledgment for every act. Or you may want to emphasize that individual benefits that will accrue to her if the profile of the unit rises, and that many of the potential demands on her time will be diverted to others. If you can manage to tie all of this to some tangible benefit you know she is seeking, all the better.

For the rest of the faculty (and here's a delicate bit), you can present the proposal as an opportunity to redefine the pool of students from which the department draws and to rethink the organization of the student experience. Plant the concept of raising the student profile well in advance, and work to get the unit as a whole to adopt it as a goal. Let it be someone else's idea. Restructure admissions and the first year of graduate experience to include rotations so that students get to work with a number of faculty members. Start a jointly staffed seminar. But work on making the drag on the star (hassling with too many applicants all the time) into a benefit for the unit as a whole. And let the star privately feel smug about the improvements.

Initiatives of this nature can be risky. It's possible that your packaging of the situation won't convince your star, or others on the faculty, to see things your way. But such initiatives also have the potential to yield payoffs not achievable in any other fashion. If the issue isn't the quality of students, you may be able to highlight your star in a seminar series, or in fundraising. Maybe your star would be good at—and feel good about—charming potential donors into endowing a facility that everyone in your unit could use, or pursuing some other high-profile activity that would benefit both the star and the rest of the department. Maybe there are deficits in the department that you can somehow capitalize upon. It's well worth spending some time thinking about things in this inside-out way.

Resource Constraints

Every academic institution always has more in mind that it wants to accomplish than its resources permit. Most department heads feel "poor" and particularly feel that they do not have enough funds to reward and recognize people appropriately. Whatever your resource base, hold in mind how much most people want to be seen as successful and to receive approval. As an academic administrator, you control resources that indicate success and approval. Many of these are not monetary, and they can even be intangible. If you orient yourself to thinking of such rewards as forms of remuneration as real as salaries, and if you learn to use them strategically, you will dramatically expand your area of positive influence.

What are the signs, in your department, that a faculty member is in favor? If someone is a rising star, is she invited to serve on the seminar committee? Included in dinners with faculty candidates? Asked to the dean's sherry party? Introduced to visiting celebrities? Is his picture posted on the bulletin board? Is her name on her letterhead? These are just a few of the perquisites that can count as coin of the realm. And you can bet that every member of your faculty, most of the graduate students, all the department's secretaries, and a fair number of other members of your staff know where each and every person stands in the pecking order as indicated by the intangible rewards.

Universities have remarkably few levels of rank, and productive faculty members achieve them fairly early in their working lives: the first promotion comes six or seven years out of graduate school, and the next (final) promotion within several years after that. Unless your university has a robust system of endowed chairs and other awards, the remaining rewards are almost all external to the institution and/or intangible. You should, of course, be sure to spend time and effort on nominating your good people for external recognition, but you should also award *and withhold* the intangible signs of favor in a strategic and purposeful way.

Don't have many such signs? Create some. Start a "tradition" of buying a new chair for the year's most prolific publisher or the faculty member with the most diverse group of graduate students. If you can't afford a new office chair, make a special bulletin board or put an orange sticker by the person's name in the faculty roster in the main office. Equally important is that you never, never give that intangible reward to someone who is not contributing to the articulated goals and values of the department. Think about how much praise means. Practice creative recognition. And withhold praise and recognition from the bad actors.

It's harder than you think, but also vastly more effective than you may anticipate.

Professors Foster and Strasse

What does all this information about the special challenges of the academic environment have to do with the way you're going to handle the problems of Foster and Strasse? Let's look first at the easier case, Professor Strasse. You've already talked with him at least once about the complaints from students and parents about his intermixing of classic nudes with his calculus lessons and his less-than-civil responses to the students who have objected. Now it's time to escalate your response. First, be sure you aren't sending him any mixed messages about his conduct. Since you've received a number of complaints about his interactions with students, make sure you don't place him on your admissions committee or any interview committees. If he has asked to move to the department's newly equipped high-tech classroom, do not grant his request while these matters are unresolved. Doing so would send the wrong message: that he can generate complaints and wave off your concerns and still get what he wants. All too often in academia, department heads think they are sending discouraging signals when, in fact, they are sending mixed or even reinforcing signals for behavior that is detrimental. Be alert to the messages your actions are sending and align them so they are consistent.

You may or may not have sufficient information about the complaints against Professor Strasse. Seek support from your administrative structure about the proper way to document student and parental complaints and bring them to a faculty member's attention, and what, if any, procedures must be invoked or discussed with the students. Strasse has the right to receive and to respond to the complaints under any concept of fairness: now is the time to give him the chance to do so, in writing.

If, as is often the case, students (or their parents) are concerned about retaliation, sort through the complaints and see if any of them are from students from previous terms whose evaluations and grades are already complete. Use your institution's prescribed process (policy and procedures can be your friends.) and start sending consistent messages that you take these matters seriously and that respectful interactions are not negotiable items in your environment. Withhold whatever rewards you properly can while the matter is pending (seek legal or administrative advice before doing this). It's perfectly reasonable to withhold the annual teaching award from a faculty member against whom more than fifteen complaints about abuse of students are pending—if you follow the proper procedure in so doing, and if you document and process the complaints in accordance with that procedure. If existing procedures do not allow you to withhold the award, consider whether you can, in good conscience, sign the nomination papers, or whether you will simply forward them without your signature. Consider the symbolic as well as the explicit communication of your acts.

Although Sally Smithson's situation looks more complicated (sex always complicates things), remember that, at least at the moment, you have no direct information about it. What you have is on the level of gossip—however well founded—because the three faculty members who have spoken to you are not in a position to stand behind their comments. Having promised not to break Smithson's confidence, they cannot admit having told you. But this is no time to play ostrich. As tempting as it may be to ignore the gossip, you will be putting yourself and your university at legal risk if you give in to that temptation. In legal parlance, you have been put "on notice" (see Chapter 6 for more details), and ignoring what you have heard will result in even worse problems.

That Smithson has apparently taken her complaint to the Office of Women's Programs and the Ombudsperson only reinforces the requirement that you deal with this. Multiple offices of the university have received reports of a problem that, if Smithson is telling the truth, is potentially serious. In addition, the fact that a large (and growing) number of people know about the allegations means that not addressing them will leave Foster in a situation from which his reputation may never recover, even if the story being told is completely untrue. Think about it: fully one-fifth of the members of your department have heard this allegation against Foster, so a large percentage of the colleagues who will vote on his promotion now have Smithson's rendition of his exploits in their heads.

Regardless of the legalities, which are lurking everywhere in this situation, simple concepts of fairness should guide your actions. Consider the golden rule: if multiple people were complaining about *you* to your evaluating supervisor, would you feel that adequate grounds for action existed? Not likely.

The first order of business is to hear or see the problem for yourself. However contrived it may need to be, arrange to meet with Ms. Smithson, and ask her how things are going. Give her a chance to speak to you directly. Ditto Dr. Foster. In a situation with this many complexities, and one that rests solely upon the credibility of two people, direct information will be invaluable.

When you have these two conversations, if either or both put the topic on the table with you, your next steps will be more straightforward, and probably guided by the university's sexual harassment procedure. If Smithson persists in her refusal to invoke that procedure, however, you may face the odious task of having to ask Foster directly whether he had a sexual relationship with her. No aspect of that conversation will be pleasant, and you should approach it only with clear coaching and advice from your institution's legal staff. One possible outcome here is that both parties will deny any sexual relationship and thus there will be no basis for invoking university procedures for review or investigation. In that circumstance—absent a formal complaint or any other evidence of wrongdoing—you and your colleagues may not properly consider any aspect of Smithson's reports as you prepare to vote on Foster's tenure.

You're not off the hook yet. Because of the concept of being "on notice," you may have still one more unwanted task before you: a conversation—followed up in writing—in which you describe to Foster the university's policy on sexual relationships with students and let him know that, should any allegation that he has violated this policy ever be received and substantiated, he will be subject to discipline that might possibly include dismissal from the university. Your side of the conversation should go something like this: "Tom, I don't have any allegations of misconduct on your part. It is my duty, though, to inform you about the university's policy on sexual relationships with students . . . [The possible consequences of violating the policy go here.] Here is a copy of the policy. I will confirm our conversation in writing." The reason for taking this step is to provide legal protection for you and the university by making sure that there can be no question about institutional policy or consequences of its violation.

You may be tempted to avoid this interaction by, for example, inviting the university's sexual harassment trainer to do a presentation at which attendance by the entire department is mandatory, and then documenting that you have done so. But imagine the dynamics of that meeting. First, by that time everyone in the department will probably have heard the rumors about the relationship between Foster and Smithson, and will know they are the reason for the presentation. Second, those whose conduct has always been correct will resent the time spent at the meeting and will feel that they are, in effect, being punished for the supposed misdeeds of Tom Foster.

Even after you gather direct information from the parties involved, this is not going to be easy to resolve. I hope it's clear, by now, that this kind of problem is not suited to informal handling—that you need to move it into the world of policy and procedure. Consider the worst-case scenario: Smithson never lodges a formal complaint, yet her story is true. And Foster later does it again: has a sexual relationship with one of his students. That woman does complain, and she uses the previous case, in which you did nothing, as evidence of a pattern of institutional indifference. She may well recover from the university, and you're likely to be sued personally along with the institution.

I'll have more to say later about the particular aspects of this situation that demand that you not attempt to resolve it informally, but for now, take it on faith: you need direct information, policy and legal support, strict adherence to procedure, and strong personal boundaries to keep this matter from being more costly than you can afford in terms of lost sleep and your stomach lining.

Chapter 3

Negotiation

Your department has been hit hard by budget cuts and is down in faculty strength more than is comfortable for sustaining your curriculum and graduate program. You are struggling with morale, trying to combat the idea that the department is a sinking ship. This is difficult, given that just this year you've had to reduce copying allocations, cancel your newsletter and seminar series, start charging faculty for long-distance calls, and stop buying equipment of any sort. There are only two bright spots: you've gotten permission from the dean to open a lateral search (the dean will pay for the line), and you've won a hard-fought battle for your faculty to be eligible for funding from the campus pool for scholarly travel. Your faculty members will have to apply for funds, but any who are speaking at conferences are guaranteed at least partial funding.

You have a meeting in ten minutes with Professor Honcho, the head of another department that occupies the building that adjoins yours. This "nontraditional" hire was brought in with great fanfare and at great expense; he holds an endowed position and has more personal discretionary funding than your whole department. The donor, a self-educated supermarket king, is big on "reforming" higher education, and has given many speeches lauding Honcho as one who will lead the way for the entire university to get over its outdated and overly PC ways. From friends and colleagues you have heard only negative reports about Honcho. They say he doesn't know or care about your university's traditions and policies and never hesitates to remind people of his program's visibility and funding.

The topic of the meeting is a request you have repeatedly turned down to relinquish your only large, high-tech classroom for use by Professor Honcho's department on Thursday afternoons in the 4–6 P.M. time slot. This room is heavily used afternoons and evenings every day of the week, and usually on weekends as well. Two months ago Honcho's assistant called to ask you to let his department use your room for its showcase seminar series. This series draws a lot of big name speakers from outside academia, such as CEOs and journalists, and gets much attention. Since the room was fully booked for classes, you couldn't grant the request, and you thought that would be the end of the matter.

But it was only the beginning. Since then you have been bombarded with email and phone calls, first from Honcho's assistant, then from the professor himself. He has suggested that you move your Thursday afternoon classes to his department's building so the highly visible seminars can be held in the high-tech classroom. No one has claimed that the seminars actually require the high-tech facilities; the argument is just that it would make the university look good for the activity to be in your better-looking room, and that you should be willing to do this for the sake of the university.

Henry Fonda's character in the movie *12 Angry Men* sways eleven initially opposed jurors—all ready to convict and anxious to escape the small and stiflingly hot jury room—to his point of view. He doesn't do it by lecturing or trying to persuade them; he starts by letting them talk, by listening, and by making sure he understands their perspectives. Then he wins them over one by one. When repeatedly challenged about whether he believes the young defendant is innocent, he says "I don't know" or "I just want to talk about it." By not taking a position, he leaves room for discussion. Track down the film and watch it with an eye to his tactics, as the astute sense of human nature demonstrated in action is worth studying. Research in social psychology affirms and explains many of the techniques Fonda's character uses. He lets people come to their own conclusions by asking questions and giving them room, and he does so without dominating the conversation. It's a masterly illustration of many of the techniques that are most effective at influencing others. Watch it more than once.

Why? Because the most important skills for any administrator are effective, professional communication and influencing techniques. You may have the best ideas in decades for your department, but unless you can bring others along with you, you might as well have none. You'll find that much of your administrative life is one negotiation after another, and negotiation requires effective listening, speaking, and influencing skills.

We all negotiate every day, with our families, our friends, and our colleagues. Some of the negotiations are such an integral part of every day life that we may not realize that we are, in fact, negotiating.

How did you decide where to have lunch with your friend last week, or where and with whom to have Thanksgiving dinner? When your teenager could use the car or what time she had to be home? Unless you have an unusually compliant set of friends and relatives who always automatically agree with you, you participated in some form of negotiation in each of these situations.

We're more accustomed to thinking about negotiation as a part of our work lives: we think of union contracts, arrangements with sponsors, or landing the new faculty member without breaking the budget. Very often we think of handling negotiations as someone else's job—the lawyers or the technology transfer agents or the human resources department. But think about how many people you interact with daily who don't see eye to eye with you, or who want something from you, or who want you to agree with them. Each of these interactions is a negotiation.

Negotiation Skills

The most important thing to know about negotiating is that it is a skill, and one that can be taught. There's a tremendous body of knowledge and research about the theory and practice of negotiation, and much of it is easily understood and applied, even by people who do not think of themselves as "negotiators." At base, an able negotiator is simply anyone who can influence the outcome of interactions with other people. Understanding the dynamics of negotiation, the importance of advance preparation, and some of the basic skills can help you do that.

Change Your Behavior

The good news and the bad news about improving your skill in negotiation are the same: in order to influence others you must change your own conduct. Think about it: you cannot *force* others to change; in a highly charged situation, the only factor you truly control is your own behavior. And changing your behavior—for example, learning to curb your impulse for direct confrontation in favor of patience and a low-key approach—can have a powerful effect on the outcome.

You can work on changing your approach, rewriting the script you'll follow in difficult conversations, entirely in private. The goal is to learn to influence others without making them lose any dignity, face, or goodwill. When you apply the new script in interactions, the most notable feature of your success may be that no one ever notices or is able to articulate the change, but that things move more smoothly and with less friction and at less cost to you.

Think of the most defensive, least responsive person you deal with regularly. Summon up your most recent truly unproductive interaction with that person, one that left you fuming or thinking of what you *should* have said even hours later. Now, replay this situation, and try to recognize the key points in the dynamic as it developed. (If you're not comfortable with this kind of visualization, notice the dynamic in your next actual encounter with this person instead.) This time, instead of engaging the same way you did before, stay calm and commit yourself to do nothing more than ask questions for at least the first two or three minutes: Not charged questions like "Have you changed your mind about the such-and-such?" but questions designed to elicit information and move the interaction off whatever point of conflict has stalled it: "Can you help me understand that policy a little more clearly?" "What goal is this helping us meet?" Try saying less and listening more, and watch what happens.

Let's take that idea and connect it with the concept of assuming a professional role consciously and with a clear understanding of its requirements and boundaries. Your role as department head requires that you set the tone, including establishing consistent expectations for successful and appropriate professional conduct, and that you provide sincere compliments for conduct that meets those expectations.

The catch is that you must be comfortable being the authority figure—or at least be able to act as if you're thoroughly comfortable in the role. To be the authority figure in an antiauthoritarian environment like the academic world takes a special touch. To do so in a positive, not dictatorial way is even trickier. All the more reason to examine your own behavior ahead of time and consider the persona you'll need for your professional role as leader of your department.

Now for a recommendation that may surprise you. You can learn a great deal about how to be an effective leader by reading books on effective parenting. If you have children, some of these books may already be on your shelves. If you're not a parent and prefer not to read about being one, the dog training literature is also a good place to learn the skills you'll need.

No, no, I am *not* suggesting that you treat your colleagues and subordinates like children or dogs. The reason to read books about good parenting or dog training is that they teach you how to modify your behavior and to build effective communication skills. They suggest practical ways to improve your listening and to ensure that your words and actions send a consistent—rather than mixed—message. Have you ever seen parents who, when their child misbehaves, keep saying, "Junior, stop that or you'll be in trouble," but don't take any action? The child, not surprisingly, ignores the admonitions and continues to misbehave. Your voice, too, is likely to be ignored if you don't use the communication skills the best books in these areas teach.

Choose to Listen

The single most powerful way to increase your influence on others in your daily negotiations is to learn to listen more effectively, more intensely, and more genuinely. Like other changes in your behavior, this is something you control entirely, and it's a change you can make on your own, which others may not notice even while they respond to it. But it can have far-reaching effects in your professional life.

Before we go on, let me say that it's easy to read what follows and nod your head without really absorbing it or making any changes. You'll probably recognize some of the ideas as ones you've seen before but never put into practice. If you really want not just to survive but to thrive as an administrator, don't do that. Slow down. Actually practice some of what's suggested here. Think about it, then practice it some more. Let me repeat: nothing will increase your ability to influence others more powerfully than improving your listening skills. It's hard work and requires continuing (frequently tedious) effort. And it makes a dramatic difference.

In general, we don't listen very well. Listening is a skill that most of us are neither taught nor practice. Instead, we "listen ahead" (jump to conclusions) while people are talking, prepare our rebuttals, think our own thoughts, and generally skim over the surface of conversations. And we reinforce our habit of not listening by social conventions in which we speak to one another but have no intention of listening: "Hi, how are you?" "Fine, and you?" Also, we often give people different levels of attention depending on their status in our lives. You probably listen more carefully to the dean than you do to the parking lot attendant—and without question, people low on your pecking order know you don't really listen to them. But how effectively are you listening even to the dean?

Listening is more complicated than it seems. We can think, and thus process spoken language, faster than people speak. As demonstrated by experiments that speed up recorded speech by omitting all the "micro-pauses," Americans talk at about 120–150 words per minute, but we can comprehend speech even at 400–500 words per minute. That leaves a lot of time in any conversation for thinking our own thoughts or anticipating what will happen next instead of truly attending to what the other person is saying. And, in our speeded-up lives, we rarely sit down and devote time to understanding and "hearing." In consequence, we leap to a lot of conclusions and *think* we know more about what others are trying to say to us than we actually do.

Try an experiment: initiate a conversation with a friend on a topic about which you disagree. Spend the first two minutes listening carefully (without taking notes), not responding substantively to anything said but instead making only "passive listening" responses intended to draw the person out: "Really?" "How so?" "Tell me more about it." At the end of the two minutes, tell the friend that you'd like to be sure you understand his perspective, and repeat the points he made—revising what you say until he agrees that you do understand. Now tell your friend what you were doing, and, if he is still game, reverse roles and this time, you be the speaker.

If you're like most people, you'll find that listening, when you know in advance that you'll have to repeat the other person's points, is much more work than holding forth on your own views. Ask yourself how often you listen to others with that level of concentration. For most of us, it's not very often.

Start small, but consciously work to adjust your listening, especially in conversations where you are the party with greater authority or power. Concentrate on what the speaker is saying; make eye contact and signal that you're listening by nodding and "uh-huhing." Do this especially with people you do not like, as you are far more likely to have telegraphed your opinions to them than to those you do like.

When an interaction starts to become contentious or involve disagreements, try the "two-minute technique," doing nothing but listening at first and then repeating the other person's views before you talk about your own opinion. "Let me make sure I understand what you're saying: your view is that . . ."

Just this small change in your approach to conversations can have far-reaching ripple effects in the way people react to you; it can smooth your interactions. And that's without applying any "mirroring" techniques for verbal or nonverbal interactions, techniques that can also decrease the friction in your daily interactions and improve your ability to influence others.

Mirroring involves becoming more aware of body language—your own and that of others. Make it a habit to watch and think about the body language you see in meetings and other workplace interactions. See if you can pick out someone who is "closed" or opposed to an idea by the way she's sitting (arms crossed, pushed back or turned away from the table), and choose that person as a target for special listening. See if the listening alone makes a difference in her body orientation to you or to the rest of the group. More often than not, it will.

Beyond just listening with closer attention, try matching the way you sit in a one-on-one conversation with the way the other person is sitting; see if this signal of being in accord facilitates communication. Also try mirroring the person's style of speaking: if she tends to use visual language ("I see what you mean"; "Can you picture it?"), use similar metaphors or the same approach when you speak. If she uses aural language ("I hear you"; "Let me hum a few bars for you"), adopt that kind of language yourself.

Why do any of this? Because being heard, being understood, is a surprisingly strong and basic human need that is all too rarely met, and shaping your own verbal and nonverbal communication to match another person's sends a signal that you do hear and understand her. You will be far more likely to influence others in your daily negotiations if they feel heard by you.

But isn't this manipulative? Isn't it phony? It can be. Much depends on the attitude you bring to it. If you are merely *pretending* to listen more carefully, as a way to manage or manipulate people, their hypocrisy detectors will pick that up. But if you sincerely seek information from them—and you probably know less than you think you do about exactly what their views are and what motivates them, and almost certainly you know less than you think about the life experiences that brought them to that point—you will not telegraph superficiality. The trick is, you truly have to listen and pay attention to what others say, and you have to process it through your brain, not just *act* as if you're listening. By giving others the gift of attention and hearing, you not only seem more congenial to them but are very likely to learn something useful—and, if nothing else, you buy yourself more time to think.

Ask Questions

You are in a situation where you must say no to a request, and you're annoyed by the gall of the colleague who is pushing the issue. You find yourself (only in your head, of course) attributing the request to selfishness, shortsightedness, or malice. This not only is a negative way to approach this transaction but is likely to pollute your future interactions with the person. Try instead to step back mentally and ask questions to elucidate both your colleague's position on the issue under discussion and the interests that underlie his position. I'll have more to say later in this chapter about the importance of focusing on people's interests when negotiating. For now, just a quick definition: positions are *what* people want, and interests are *why* they want them.

Start with very simple, open-ended questions, the kind recommended by high school journalism teachers: Why? What? How?

- Why do you want that? Why does that solve the problem?
- What are your concerns? What, exactly, is the problem?
- How does this address your interests? How does it affect others?

Consider that you cannot truly understand a situation if you don't know these basics—and do not substitute your surmises for information provided by the other person. Ask, and then apply your listening skills when the person replies.

Follow the advice of the negotiation guru William Ury: strive for a real curiosity about the other person's perspective—especially if you think you already know all about it. Put aside your preconceptions. Listen intently; force yourself to slow down and use what the parenting books call "active listening." In active listening, you repeat portions of what others say to be sure you've heard it correctly. If you don't like the formulaic "So I hear you saying such and such," simply echo a few key points others have made, or say something like "Let me make sure I understand what you mean" and then briefly rephrase what you've heard. (This is also a good way to cut off a tirade without giving offense: people aren't likely to be offended if you interrupt them for the purpose of making sure you understand *their* point, and if you can repeat their point accurately—even if you then add some points of your own.) See if you can repeat not only the person's request but also the reasons and basis for it. If you can, you'll have accomplished an important step in negotiation tactics by focusing on interests, not positions.

Do Your Homework

Now that you know about the importance of changing your own behavior, working on your listening skills, and asking questions to gather information, you're ready for another crucial element of good negotiation: preparation. (After all, good listening is necessary but not sufficient: you could become a great listener and still cave in every time you listen.) We are all too prone to wing it—to walk into an interaction and respond spontaneously. A prepared negotiator is a more effective negotiator. Negotiation is not something that either comes intuitively or doesn't come at all. We all have varying degrees of comfort with conflict (to be negotiating, you have to have some kind of difference or conflict with the other person) or disagreement or haggling. But since you are going to be negotiating whether you like it or not, why not do what you can to become more effective than you are now? Careful advance preparation can dramatically increase your chances of getting the outcome you want.

Part of your preparation we've already discussed: knowing yourself; becoming more aware of your role as an authority figure and your goals for your role and your term of service. Another key step is to recognize when an interaction *is* a negotiation: this isn't just one more hallway conversation. When someone comes to you and asks for something you haven't thought about yet, don't want to give, cannot give, or even were planning to give but not under these circumstances, stick a mental tag on the interaction and think "Aha, we're negotiating."

When you know in advance that you're going to have to negotiate (say, with the dean about the budget), you probably do some homework, getting the facts and figures together and marshaling your arguments. Thorough preparation involves more homework than that.

Not only must you know what you want (and what you could live with) and why, you must make a conscious and concentrated effort to think through the interests of other party to the negotiation. Yes, you'll be able to ask questions about interests during the negotiation itself, but the more you can find out about them in advance, the better. What is motivating the dean? What are her interests? Think about the pressures she has to deal with. What makes her look good? What are the easy things for her to grant if she doesn't have the money you've requested? What are her stated goals? How can you frame your wants or needs as things that will contribute to her goals? How does what you want fit into her big picture, with all the requests she gets from others? If you haven't given careful thought to her interests in this situation (other than avoiding yet another meeting where all she does is make people unhappy), you are not prepared for the negotiation.

The same is true when a person wants something from you: if you have not thought about that person's interests, you are not prepared. Suppose a faculty member asks you to change the classroom assignments so he can teach in a particular room. Give some careful thought to what may be motivating his request, and prepare some questions in advance to get him to tell you his reasons. Once you know the *why* behind what he's asking, you can go on to problem-solving that addresses the underlying interests he has articulated. And then either you'll find a solution (or an acceptance of the situation), or perhaps you'll find that he's shifting the grounds for his request and is now presenting different reasons. If you see that happening, you may want to (with good humor) suspend the discussion until another day to give him time to think about what he really wants and why.

Putting yourself in the other person's shoes and imagining the situation from his perspective is vital to your preparation for any negotiation. This is a skill that may not come naturally at first and may even feel alien; your impulse may be to focus on the flaws of the other's position. Practice it until it does feel natural. You can't really know the flaws in his position until you fully understand the position itself and the reasons behind it. Think it through on your own; prepare questions to elicit more information; ask the questions; and *listen* to the answers.

Identify Interests

After listening, one of the most important things to learn about negotiating is to focus on people's interests rather than their positions. Disputes that get hung up on positions can easily escalate into power struggles and aggressive exchanges. If you cultivate the skill of steering conversations back to interests, your professional life will go more smoothly and your interactions will be more productive.

You already know the key to doing that: asking questions and listening to the responses. Research has shown that effective negotiators ask more questions than less effective negotiators do. In particular, effective negotiators use questions to learn about others' interests.

There are two overall types of negotiation. In the distributive or "win-lose" type, one issue (usually money) is at stake, it's divisible, and the parties have no long-term relationship with one another. Most of the negotiations in our daily and professional lives are of the other sort: integrative negotiations, in which more than one issue is stake, continuing relationships exist between the parties, and the parties may assign different values to the issues. In such circumstances, persistently focusing on interests—asking many sincere questions to draw out the *whys* of the matter and to understand the perspective of the other party—leaves much more room for what have come to be known as "win-win" situations, in which both parties feel they have gained something from a negotiation and the relationship is preserved.

Once you know the *whys* of an issue—people's reasons for wanting what they want—you can fashion a solution that responds to those reasons that both sides may find more palatable than continuing to clash over something irresolvable.

For example, let's go back to the request from a faculty member to change the room assignment of one of his seminars. You know he is not willing to teach at a different time, and you know the room he prefers will not be available at the time of his seminar, because it will be occupied by a course from another unit of the university that has priority over your department. Or because the room accommodates up to sixty students, and large classes have priority over seminars. Or because it has high-tech equipment and thus is reserved for courses that actually use the technology, but he only uses transparencies on the overhead projector. Or for any of a multitude of other reasons.

Before you throw up your hands and say "Sorry, not possible" (which he may well hear as "I won't do this for you because you're not in favor"), ask questions. Try to find out what it is about the room that appeals to him: proximity to his office because he has to carry heavy materials to class? The layout of the room? Once you know what pedagogical (or personal) needs the room would serve for him, you can start focusing on working *together* to solve his problem: What if we let you use the department's rolling cart to get your heavy items to and from class? Or what if students helped you carry them? What if you could use the conference room for your seminar? What if you could help plan next year's remodeling of the classroom you're assigned to? What if we increased the enrollment in your seminar or you taught another class to more students, thus qualifying to use the larger room?

Don't go into this conversation with a closed mind, assuming that his reason for wanting the room is petty or invalid: to keep someone he doesn't like from getting it; to assert himself over you, his new boss; or some such motive. And don't go into it with the attitude that the room simply isn't available so the issue is closed. Whatever his motivation, if you can shape the conversation as one in which you are seeking information so that the two of you can try to solve the problem together, you can give the interaction a positive tone. Even if he doesn't get the room he wants, he may get something else that matters to him, and if he feels you have genuinely listened to his concerns, he will leave your office with more positive feelings about you and the outcome than if you simply convey the message "No, I can't let you use the room, and you should stop asking."

Accomplishing the shift in mind-set from "I'm going to win" to "How can we both come out of this interaction with things we need?" is a major conceptual move and an essential one. When I teach negotiation to law students, I spend the first third of the semester working on resetting their adversarial mind-set to one in which they seek ways to resolve disputes and make deals that let both parties feel at least somewhat positive about the outcome. If you practice this approach until you are good at it and comfortable with it, you will discover not only that you'll find acceptable solutions to many problems, but also that simply hearing people respectfully and being willing to work *with* them will make some problems go away. "I know you really can't assign me that room, but this whole situation just gets up my nose. Thanks for your time."

As Roy Lewicki, a leading scholar of negotiation, points out, a negotiation at its most basic level is a conversation. It occurs between two or more people who have some kind of conflict or difference, and who come together voluntarily with at least a mild preference for a negotiated resolution. And in a negotiation both parties expect some give and take: research shows that people feel better about the outcome of a transaction—even when it is not the outcome they wanted—if the other party made some concessions from the starting point. Because negotiations are conversations between people, in any negotiation you must attend to and manage the intangible, relationship-based elements as well as the issue under dispute. Intangibles include feelings about "winning," saving face, the precedents involved, levels of trust, reputations, concepts of fairness, and so on. If you are not aware of these issues beneath the surface, you will be at a disadvantage in the interaction.

Stages of Negotiation

Yes, negotiations are conversations, but they are structured: they go through a series of specific stages. (Experts in negotiation characterize the stages in different ways; I follow the sequence articulated by Charles Craver, a specialist in legal negotiation who was one of my teachers when I was in law school.) While you may have an impulse to jump right into the haggling stage (the give-and-take bargaining), there are three other stages that you should take care to go through sequentially before you get to the heart of the matter. Skipping the preliminary stages is not a good idea, even in interactions with people you know well.

The Opening Stage: Honey, Not Vinegar

The most overlooked part of a successful negotiation happens at the very beginning. At this point your goal should be to build rapport and set the tone for what follows. You want to chat pleasantly for a short time before bringing up anything substantive. Establishing a human connection at the beginning is very important to positive outcomes. It is a fact of human nature that we give more to people we like than to people we don't like. Think about it: How hard do you find it to agree with someone you have disliked for years? It's usually much harder than agreeing with someone you like and respect. When we like people and feel comfortable with them, we find it less threatening to explore novel approaches or to be open to new ideas, so problem solving is easier.

If you can keep in mind that, especially in the long-term professional connections that often characterize university departments, the *relationship* matters as much as the individual issue, you'll be ahead of the game in persuading people and doing well in negotiations. Cultivate likeability. Civility and cordiality are often undervalued in this world, where too many people think the most effective way to achieve their goals is through aggressive conduct. As our grandmothers knew, you catch more flies with honey than with vinegar.

Stage Two: Collecting Information

After you've established (or reestablished) the human connection, you have yet another step to take before the bargaining begins. This is the time to find out what the other party wants, and most important, to discover the *whys*.

It may seem counterintuitive, but the key to resolving problems often lies in the differences we bring to the table: differences between the parties in values, priorities, and needs create fruitful ground for problem solving, or, in negotiation terms, for making the pie bigger for everyone.

Take the classic distributive (win-lose) negotiation: buying a car from a dealer you do not know. Every extra dollar you pay is an extra one in the dealer's pocket. You may dread haggling over price and have a history of simply paying whatever the dealer asks, or offering whatever *Consumer Reports* says is the average consumer price for the car. You may imagine that the pie is a fixed size and that the dealer will do the cutting and serving, leaving you with the smallest piece. This is the kind of negotiation in which doing your homework really matters and your listening skills will get a good workout.

Stage Three: Value for Both Parties

Even the negotiation between you and the car dealer can be converted into one with integrative (win-win) elements, if you seek information about the dealer's interests (other than getting as much money out of you as possible) and figure out where you and the dealer have *differences*. The goal is to add issues to the negotiation to make the pie a little bigger.

So, for example, if you know when car dealers must pay taxes on

their inventory, it's reasonable to assume that they are more motivated to sell the cars on the lot just before that date. You've just
added an immediate sale as an issue in the negotiation. If you notice
that a dealer has a surplus of cars of a certain color, and if you care
more about price than about color, you've discovered a difference
that may expand the pie further so that each of you can have a
larger piece: the dealer may be able to unload a color that isn't selling well, and you may save some money. Sellers often exploit buy-
ers' cravings for immediate gratification: you can take a car that's on
the lot right now, but you'll have to wait for one with the features
you've listed. That's a difference in valuations of time. So, for example, if you walk into the showroom knowing that the car dealer's
inventory taxes are due in a few days, and if you've seen a large
number of black cars on the lot, your knowledge of the dealer's interests may give you some leverage for reducing the price.

What other interests might the dealer have? If you've bought
other cars from him in the past, your negotiation has moved out of
the classic one-issue distributive model, because the two of you
have a longer-term relationship. That's an additional issue that
makes the pie bigger. Many car dealers are trained to ask you about
yourself as a way to build affinity, so you'll find them likeable and
be more amenable to their persuasion: "Oh, you went to Big U? So
did my wife." "You're a cat lover? I have a couple of Siamese my-
self." Be alert to that tactic, and also think about whether you can
use some variation of it to your advantage. The dealer probably has
an interest in his reputation in the area, and in future sales. Is there
anything you can do that would be of value to him and thus induce
him to grant you a further discount? To repeat: identify interests—
the other party's and your own—and note differences between the
two that may provide opportunities to create value for both of you.

Now let's translate this into the academic environment. Think about recruiting a new faculty member. In addition to money, what do you have to offer that she might value? If you've done your homework and listened well in your interactions, you should know something about her. If you're just starting the process, be sure to ask open-ended questions ("What are you looking for in your next position?") and listen to the answers. Keep track of the questions the recruit asks you (take notes!) and see if you can discern a pattern. Is the focus on colleagues? Facilities? What it will be like to live in your town? The difficulty of moving?

Do what you can to gather information about the person's interests, and then frame your recruitment in terms of those interests. Your own interests are relevant too, of course, but they aren't the ones that will drive her decision. So it's a good idea to frame your concerns in terms of complimentary things about her (we all like to hear sincere and relevant praise), such as how well her work in her subfield fits with the department's plan to build strength in that area. Similarly, the more you know about the recruit's interests, the more you can create value for her by providing information and opportunities that matter to her. Even if you can't match the largest financial package she's considering, if your approach is tailored to the interests she has expressed, you may still be able to attract her to your campus by emphasizing the good schools for her children, proximity in the building to a colleague she wants to work with, the ease of getting work done in your department, and the top-notch local running club where she could train with other serious marathoners.

Stage Four: Horse-Trading

You are ready for the haggling part of the negotiation only after you have established rapport, gleaned as much information as you can, and imagined ways to increase the size of the pie for both of you. Only then is it time to get down to dividing up the pie.

Again, put the other party's interests first when deciding how to word your offer: frame what you say in terms of the interests she has expressed, while being honest about your own interests. Remember that arguments expressed in terms of her interests will be more persuasive to her than ones expressed in terms of your own.

Many of us would prefer to believe that our positions are based entirely on facts and rational analysis, and therefore that the way to persuade others to come around to our point of view is simply to assemble a cogent enough argument. But if any of us actually *do* believe this, we're deluding ourselves. Many factors other than rationality, including our feelings about the people involved, public positions we've taken previously, and a variety of superstitions and prejudices, affect where we stand on various issues. Here I'll give you a few handy concepts that have arisen from research on negotiation.

One useful idea is known as *anchoring*. It turns out that numbers people hear during a negotiation, whether relevant or not, tend to stick in their minds and affect their perception of the value of numbers that come up later. In a famous experiment by Amos Tversky and Daniel Kahneman, college students were asked to estimate the percentage of African countries in the United Nations after watching a roulette wheel stop at pre-set numbers. Even though the numbers on the wheel clearly had nothing to do with the estimation task, those who saw the wheel stop at a higher number estimated larger percentages than those who saw the wheel stop at a lower number.

Because negotiators tend to anchor on irrelevant information, you must be vigilant. One irrelevant number that often infects negotiations is the first offer that others make to you. Your homework before a negotiation should include a clear-sighted analysis of the value of the negotiation, not only to you, but to the others involved as well, using whatever benchmarks you can find that indicate market value or value in your environment.

Another interesting tidbit from the research is that people are much more satisfied with outcomes when they feel that they have influenced the results—that they have achieved something by negotiating. For example, in simulated negotiations to settle a personal injury case, those who received a first offer of $2,000 but eventually settled for $12,000 were happier with their settlements than those who were first offered $10,000 and settled for $12,000. The outcomes were the same, but those who felt they had managed to raise the original offer more dramatically felt better in the end. If those with whom you are negotiating feel they've had an effect on the outcome—rather than being unheard or ineffectual—they will feel better about themselves, the process, and you.

These insights into the way our brains deal with numbers will be useful as you prepare for certain kinds of negotiations. In vastly oversimplified form, the advice that flows from them is that, if you have good information on the issues and their market value (or their value in your environment), it is often a good idea to make the first offer rather than wait to hear the other side's offer before speaking. These insights also suggest that in such a situation one should make the most optimistic first offer that can be justified on a principled basis. In contrast, if you do not have complete and trustworthy information, especially about the other party's interests or values, try to elicit a first offer, but don't let an extreme number anchor your own thinking. (Not sure how to elicit a first offer? Try asking. You'll be astonished by people's willingness to answer direct questions.) Don't take these suggestions as hard-and-fast rules, though; each negotiation has its own complexities, and you'll need to tailor your strategy to them.

Naturally there are many factors to consider in deciding whether and how to follow this advice. The first and foremost should be your relationship with the other party. Bear in mind that if you develop a reputation for being an extreme bargainer you'll lose both your personal credibility and the value of anchoring. So you don't want to overdo it, or to go beyond acceptable bounds for your situation and your setting. (You might say the idea is to make the most extreme first offer that's not obviously extreme.) If your dean feels that you approach every encounter as a winner-takes-all contest, without considering the longer-term context in which you both operate, you'll be at a disadvantage in every negotiation with the dean. Go back to the concept of formulating goals not just for particular interactions but for your term as an administrator and for your overall career. What pattern of relationships are you creating? When it to your advantage to let people bargain you down or up, and in what situations do you consider your decisions nonnegotiable?

For example, let's assume that you have some funds to hand out and are allocating them yourself rather than delegating the task to a committee. When responding to requests, it's worth bearing in mind the differences between requestors. If you low-ball the timid faculty member who is in awe of your (perceived) authority, he is unlikely to attempt to negotiate with you. Instead he may accept your small grant and leave feeling crushed or resentful, or he may attempt to scrape by without sufficient funding, thus possibly defeating the entire purpose of the grant. At the other end of the spectrum, if you negotiate too much with the wheeler-dealer on your faculty, you may have opened yourself up to a lifetime of having every decision second-guessed and wheedled. So it pays to think carefully about when you are willing to negotiate and when you want to send the message that what you say is what you mean. If, in your college, there are certain generally accepted issues around which negotiating is accepted and the norm (stipends for taking on burdensome duties, say, or budgets for special events), then, in those situations, make the most extreme yet principled first offers you can, in a way that is not insulting and leaves room for horse-trading. Let the others win something. But never negotiate over issues on which you expect your decisions to be accepted as final—or, much like the parent who rewards a temper tantrum in the grocery store with a candy bar, you will train people not to trust what you say.

The Final Stage: Confirm Your Agreement

Do not forget, at the end of your negotiation, to restate, aloud, the deal you believe you've made. It is remarkably easy, even when you're working hard to be explicit, for differing assumptions to lead to miscommunication. Before you conclude the transaction, say something like this: "I'm so glad you're joining us. As I understand it, then, you'll be starting this August, when the office next to Olga's will be ready for you. We'll pay your moving expenses, and [specify what else you've agreed to do]. Have I left anything out? I'll confirm all this in a letter, of course. I really think this is a place you'll be able to get great work done and join a great running club, too." Now is the time to clear up any misunderstandings to prevent your carefully negotiated deal from unraveling later.

This is also the stage at which to ask if there's anything else that would make the deal better for the other person. It's entirely possible that something she values would be easy for you to provide. She may ask if you're willing to call the parking division and get her name on the waiting list right away. She may wish her uncle could be invited to the next alumni event in his town. If so, finding out about it and adding it to her piece of the pie may make a difference in her feelings about the negotiation, pleasing her far more than it inconveniences you. This may also be the moment when you can discover whether she's willing to concede something that matters to *you*. ("Sure, I can get my acceptance back to you before Friday if having it in hand would help out with the dean.")

Whatever you do, don't gloat as you close the negotiation, even if you feel you've won an overwhelming victory. You want the other person to feel good about your deal, if for no other reason than to prevent post-negotiation second thoughts and retractions. If you're negotiating with someone with whom you'll be interacting in the future—whether you like each other or not—it's even more important to let that person leave the negotiation feeling good about it, not ground into the dirt.

Bringing It All Together

With a revised way of thinking about negotiating, improved listening skills, a commitment to thorough preparation, and some knowledge of the structure of negotiations, you are ready to start putting the pieces together. The myriad negotiations of your work life require you to master another professional skill, layering it over your instinctive reactions.

Another concept from experts on negotiation will be helpful here and in everything you do: *reframing*. We all do this when we say "Look on the bright side" or seek the silver lining. The way we frame events in our minds is pivotal: Is this a gain or a loss? Is it possible to see this as a victory instead of as a defeat? Is there some common ground we haven't identified? Is there a way to make lemonade from this pile of lemons? You can choose how to characterize adversity, conflict, differences, and mistakes—and your attitude will influence those around you.

Use reframing to think yourself and others into more constructive approaches to problems. Imagine you're in conflict with someone. There are two polar ways to conceptualize the situation. One possibility: the other party is totally off base, confused, neurotic, stupid, or just generally wrong. Another: it's possible that the other party might have a point, and that you could be mistaken or have misunderstood.

The reality is probably some combination of the two. Whichever it is, *you* are in an unpleasant interaction and—remember—the only behavior you can control is your own. So, however strongly you wish the other guy would see the error of his ways, what you get to choose is how *you* act and what *you* do. The good news is that the way you act can have a dramatic effect on the outcome of the interaction. What you should do is, first, work to defuse aggression by using good listening skills, making sure the other party feels heard and valued, and, second, use problem-solving, integrative negotiation techniques.

In short, you are going to work to build trust, ask questions, share information (in order to get information), and brainstorm together. You will search for interests (*why* the other is seeking a particular goal) instead of positions. You'll depersonalize the problem by focusing on it, not on the personalities: "This is a hard problem," *not* "They're unreasonable jerks." You'll find ways to reframe the conflict that emphasize areas of agreement, and use "and" more than "but" when you restate matters.

Now, to weave all these skills into a seamless whole, think back to how important it is to know yourself. What do you know about your approach to conflict, and what works best for you? Are you a competitor? An avoider? To thrive as a person whose professional role is to work with others, you need strong insights into your own preferences and styles for dealing with conflict. We all have different comfort levels with conflict and different reactions when challenged. There's no one right answer in this arena. The key is to know yourself well enough to avoid situations where you blow up or shut down, and to recognize the tactics used by others in a charged situation.

More than anything else, you need to be able to adjust your own responses to the situation in which you find yourself, so that they serve the goals of your term of service both immediately and in the longer term. It does no good to indulge in the quick gratification of slash-and-burn rhetoric, freezing someone out, or making the perfect cutting remark if doing so damages your relationship or your ability to achieve the goals you've set for yourself and your unit. Ask yourself whether the momentary triumph will compensate for compromising your effectiveness as a leader. If the moment is sufficient for you—perhaps it pays back for years of slights or accumulated ill will—then know that and be satisfied. On the other hand, if you have your eye on a bigger goal, then summon up what it takes to forgo that triumph and focus on the problem-solving, negotiating persona you've been cultivating as part of your leadership package: think about ways to *add* issues to expand the pie and create an integrative negotiation. Or, if all else fails, terminate the interaction so that you can return to pie-expanding, integrative negotiations another day. Don't ask the impossible of yourself . . . just preserve possibilities.

One concluding word of advice: Don't let it be about you. Focus on the principles, the problems, and the goals.

Professor Honcho's Seminars

As you prepare for your meeting with Professor Honcho, it is important to think clearly and creatively about the situation and to find ways to make it into a problem-solving negotiation. If there's a chip on your shoulder when you think of this hotshot's assumption that he can trespass on your department's territory, set it aside before the meeting begins. You may long to wax indignant about putting the university's educational mission ahead of shallower concerns like publicity. You may picture yourself giving the newcomer a much-needed lesson in institutional values and tradition. Acknowledge these impulses to yourself as part of your preparation, but don't take them with you to the meeting. Think about whether, in winning the battle, you might lose the war.

And think about whether conceding this particular battle might help you win any others. At the moment, you have something Honcho wants, and he might be willing to do something beneficial for you in return. But suppose you refuse to let him use the room for his seminar series. If in response he uses some of his department's considerable resources to remodel a space in his own building, pretty soon he won't need anything from you, and he'll no longer have any reason to do you any favors, now or in the future.

If, instead, you approach this encounter as a negotiation, you may be able to use it to create value for your department. Change your behavior (knock that chip off your own shoulder). Do your homework (know what you want and why; also look at the situation from Honcho's perspective; make a list of questions to ask him). Then, after you've listened for a while, advance some of your interests and see if there are mutually beneficial ways to proceed. For example: if he has access to resources that your department does not, are there ways his department (or resources) could help out your educational mission? Maybe he could purchase equipment for the unremodeled rooms your department would need to use, and your department could keep it? Perhaps they have a sufficiently large printing budget that they could take up printing the newsletter you had to discontinue. Or, they could invite some seminar speakers that your department would love to have but can no longer afford, in a certain number of events per year? It would be better than the none you presently have. Maybe there are other ideas that will emerge, if you give him a chance to talk with you.

He's probably not totally immune to how others have perceived him in his time at your university. Maybe, if you give him a chance, you'll actually find something to like about him. If so, and if you approach this as a negotiation involving give and take and mutual value creation, you may be able to improve your department's situation. You won't find out if you don't try.

Chapter 4

Complaints

Your undergraduate studies director tells you that students have been complaining about a certain class all semester. The number and nature of the complaints are unprecedented in his experience. The class is taught by Professor Holdover, who has held the rank of associate professor in your department for twenty-three years. His teaching evaluations have been average to low for some time, but the new complaints are unusual. The students say that he often lectures for as much as forty minutes before mentioning any material relating to the class.

The course is required, and it is a prerequisite for another required course next semester. That second course is taught by one of your top teachers, who is both dynamic and very demanding. The students worry that they are not learning enough in Professor Holdover's class to do well in the next one.

You have also heard from one of your graduate students

that a graduate seminar given by Holdover is "a complete waste of time."

Today three undergraduates came directly to your office from Holdover's class. They reported that the professor had taken offense at something a student said and had begun berating the class in a very loud voice for being "impertinent, ignorant, and irredeemable." He told them they were wasting his time and he would no longer bother lecturing to people who clearly couldn't grasp the material. He then adjourned class for ten minutes, wrote an exam, and delivered it. It covered the next three weeks' worth of material, and the students are very concerned about its effect on their grades. They think Professor Holdover was drunk or otherwise impaired.

It's a well kept secret that administrative work is a lot like raising children: if you recognize that it's your job to set the tone and the boundaries, look to the long-term outcome, and exercise patience, things go more smoothly than if you let your frustrations show. If you're cheerful and optimistic and figure that most problems can be solved, people around you will pick up that attitude, and the problems are more likely to be solved.

Listening Well

Good listening is particularly important when people are making complaints. In addition to ensuring that all participants are talking about the same things (not a trivial concern, as you will know if you have sat through meetings at which each person who speaks seems to focus on a different issue), listening carefully is a way of acknowledging that everyone has a right to be heard. People who feel they are being heard are more likely to be receptive to your responses, even when you can't give them the answers they want. You can defuse many situations by devoting time at the beginning to being sure you accurately and fully understand what each person is saying. Thus, when someone brings you a complaint, apply the complete repertoire of listening skills that you learned in Chapter 3. Use effective listening to elicit the whole story, and echo it back to be sure you understand it before you make any response or formulate any action. You may think this advice falls into the "easier said than done" category—but it is critical.

Setting Boundaries

Remember the god Janus and the importance of good boundaries? Boundaries matter at least as much when you are an authority figure receiving a complaint as in other aspects of your job. You will need boundaries for time, topics, and confidence.

Many people will seek your guidance about problems that you didn't cause and may not be able to fix. If you have the time to spend listening, that's great. But it's more likely that you'll need to set limits on the time you devote to such discussions. A useful practice is to make it clear at the outset that you have only a certain amount of time to listen right now, but that another meeting can be arranged if necessary. Offer a starting and ending time for that later meeting, too. If you are in the middle of something when someone comes to you with a problem, or if you have other obligations and cannot meet immediately, do not hesitate to ask the person to set up a later appointment. Express interest in the topic, and say you want to discuss it when you have time to give it your full attention; then excuse yourself. One good way to bring the interaction to a close is to stand up and walk the person out of your office. (If that doesn't work, consider a visit to the restroom—especially if the person is of the opposite sex. Only once in my entire career have I been followed into a women's room by a man.) Failing that option, if the situation is becoming dire, consider putting on your coat, going to your car, and doing an errand, or at least driving around the block, before you return to your office.

Beyond time-based boundaries, it's also useful to develop a concept of topical boundaries. Be wary of confusing personal and professional roles. You can be cordial and warm without offering or receiving confidences that are more appropriately shared with friends, family members, or therapists. If people come to you seeking advice on personal issues, refer them to resources such as the campus counseling service; do not take on the advice-giving role yourself. In turn, you need to establish your own boundaries and keep your personal problems out of the workplace, especially when talking to those who are lower than you on the power curve.

Bear in mind when you are receiving a complaint the importance of collecting facts as you listen. As appropriate, ask what evidence is available and get copies of whatever material the person has brought to show you. As you do so, however, take care not to violate another kind of boundary: do not convey the idea that the person should go forth and act as an independent investigator ferreting out information. It must be clear that you are taking the information as part of your complaint-receipt process, not deputizing the complainant to go on a fact-finding mission.

Finally, you need to learn the boundaries of privacy and confidences. Unhappy people will sometimes tell you things you (and they) later wish they hadn't. (How much did you really want to know about her ex-husband's peculiar sexual habits?) When that happens, you may have an impulse to talk about their situation with someone else, either to help you work out a good approach to the situation or simply to express your amazement at the range of human conduct. Curb that impulse to the maximum possible extent. If you must seek counsel, find the most discreet person you can, preferably someone outside your immediate professional context or someone who has a professional obligation to keep the confidence. Academic departments are very small communities, and even veiled comments can travel over the grapevine in ways that will be damaging both to the person who offered the confidence and to your own reputation. Cultivate a reputation for trustworthiness by keeping confidences.

There is some information, though, that you *cannot* keep confidential, no matter how you come by it, and the sooner you can come to terms with this unpleasant reality, the better. If your role requires you to act upon what you hear—for example, if someone tells you that human subjects are being mistreated in an experiment (a real example out of my own past), or that one member of your department is being sexually harassed by another—make it clear to your informant that you will be unable to keep the situation confidential. Say whom you must tell and why. Offer to protect the source only if doing so is truly within your power. More often than will be comfortable for you, it may not be.

Key Sentences

A good friend of mine prepares for every contentious meeting by deciding what her first sentence is going to be. If she knows that, she says, she can wing it from there. Picking up on her idea, let's consider some sentences that may come in handy in later parts of the discussion. Say Jerry Townsend, a staff member, comes to you with a complaint about Professor Chandler.

"What action do you seek from me?" If Jerry Townsend is extremely upset, you may need to keep repeating this question. The goal is to set boundaries on both your time and the topic, as well as to focus on the desired outcome. You may be surprised at how little he actually wants from you or how simple the problem is to resolve. If he simply needs to be heard, and neither wants nor expects you to take action, it is best to confirm that directly. Often, talking through the problem will help a person recognize a way to approach the problem him- or herself. If, however, Townsend does seek action from you, elicit the clearest possible statement of what he wants. And once you've heard it, a second sentence is often useful.

"Now that I've listened carefully to you, I need to find out what the other people involved have to say. I'll get back to you after I do that." This is an application of one of the most critical guidelines for handling complaints, namely that you should never act after hearing only one side of a story. (And sometimes, no action at all is the best response.) There are at least two sides to every story. You can stress that you have no reason not to believe what Townsend has told you, but that you have an obligation to hear more, from Professor Chandler and anyone else involved, before deciding what to do. Give Townsend some indication of when you expect to be able to get back to him—and if gathering the information takes longer than you expect, *notify him of the delay.* Ignorance breeds pessimism, and while you may know that the cause of the delay is be-

nign (you teach all day Tuesday and have a commitment that evening; Chandler teaches all day Wednesday, rushes from class to the airport, and doesn't return until Monday), Townsend, waiting in some anxiety for a response, will be imagining many malignant reasons (you didn't believe a word he said; Chandler has clout in the department and is badmouthing him . . .).

"You need to do what you need to do." Some variation of this sentence is a good response to a person—say it's Jerry Townsend again—who threatens to sue the university, or you, or everyone you ever met. Emphasize that you remain willing to work with him to resolve the problem within the department, but do nothing to indicate that you are either afraid of or seeking out a lawsuit: simply make the boundaries of your ability to act as clear as possible. It is not your job to provide advice to someone wishing to pursue legal options, or even to consult on whether to obtain legal advice. Explain that you don't handle legal complaints, and try to find out if there are other items that you and Townsend can constructively discuss. Call the university's lawyer to explain the situation as soon as the meeting is over if you think legal consequences (complaints, grievances, lawsuits) are a real possibility.

Guidelines

With the key sentences internalized and ready for use, you're ready to consider the guidelines for handling complaints.

Don't take it personally. Do not get defensive when people complain, and do not jump to conclusions about their causes or the solutions. When someone—let's say it's Professor Dalton this time—comes to you with a problem or a complaint, explore whether she actually seeks any action from you (remember the first of our key sentences) or whether talking with you will be enough for the time being. Thank her for reporting the problem—and be sincere about this: it's better you know about it than you don't, even if it turns out to be a misunderstanding—and then set about collecting the facts. Keep your demeanor cordial and courteous. Aim for understatement, not emphatic rhetoric. If you find yourself tempted to say "That's the stupidest idea I've ever heard," bite your tongue, and don't speak until you've translated your response into something softer and more appropriate to your role: "I'm not sure I understand this; will you please explain it again?"

Remember that in your administrative role you may need to handle issues you would prefer to ignore. While some problems may go away if ignored, the serious ones rarely do. And those are almost always more easily resolved when caught early. Thus you need to find out what Professor Dalton is seeking as economically as possible (in time as well as emotional energy), determine who is the appropriate person to act (if action is called for at all), and use our second key sentence: "I need to find out how the other people involved perceive . . ." Then go on to the next step, one I've mentioned before.

Never act on a complaint without hearing (at least) two sides to the story. Most complaints and problems stem from different perceptions of the same situation or subsets of the same facts. Arm yourself with as complete a sense of the circumstances as you can get before you commit to a course of action. Do not accuse people when you ask; simply inform them in a low-key way that a problem has been brought to your attention and you need to collect basic information about it.

What "everybody knows," nobody knows. This is a corollary to the preceding precept. If Professor Dalton tells you about a problem and asserts that "everybody knows" it is happening, this is a good time to start asking how she herself learned about it, and also for dates, times, places, and the names of other people who have relevant information. It is remarkable how many widely known "truths" have no factual basis, but are instead rooted in an adult version of the children's game "telephone." That's the game in which one person whispers a sentence to another, who passes it along to the next, until the last person in the chain says it out loud: rarely is the final version very similar to the original sentence. Be wary of anything "everybody knows."

When in doubt, leave it out. If the sentence about to come out of your mouth begins "I know you won't like hearing this, but . . . ," or if your better judgment tells you not to say something, don't say it. This rule also applies to written communication. Short is better than long in contentious situations. The more words you offer, the more there is to nitpick. Emphasize facts and decisions, ask quiet questions, and avoid explanations of motives.

Never attribute to malice that which incompetence will explain. We are far too quick to attribute bad motives to others: most of the time, bad things happen through inattention, inaction, or miscommunication. (Social psychologists have a wonderful term for this—

the "sinister attribution bias.") Quite often, we haven't understood. The first step when concerned about a situation is to ask for clarification: "Is this right?" "I'm not sure I understand; can you help me?" "How does this fit with our decision to do X?" Another useful technique is to repeat what you have heard the person say until you get it right. Remember your listening skills? Bring them out now. Sometimes miscommunication is complicating the situation. At other times, more rarely in my experience, something is truly amiss and requires action. But asking first, and applying the golden rule ("Do unto others as you would have others do unto you"), will resolve an extraordinary number of apparent problems.

Say what you'll do and do what you say; set the time frame. Once you've decided upon a course of action, even if it's just to talk to various people to gather information, follow through on it. Nothing will compromise your credibility more than to make commitments you do not fulfill or to declare boundaries you do not enforce. Just as some parents unintentionally train their children to have temper tantrums in grocery stores by offering them candy bars if they'll calm down, you too will train people to behave inappropriately if you show them that by doing so they can get you to bend or break announced rules.

For example, every now and then you may encounter a person who has become a committed filer of grievances—who seeks every possible waiver or exception and makes every rebuff the basis for a formal grievance. If, out of exhaustion or a wish for a simple solution, you grant an exception or a waiver to such a person when you normally would not, you may find that you have simply reinforced the habit of filing grievances and made your job harder rather than easier.

In the absence of facts, people make them up. Ignorance breeds pessimism. That is, when people are worried or distraught, they usually imagine things that are worse than the reality. Don't leave them hanging, waiting for a response, for long periods of time. (The definition of a "long" period of time will vary proportionately with how upset the person is.) Form the practice of telling people what steps you will take, when you will get back to them, and that you will notify them if the time frame shifts. Then stick to your word. You may also want to invite them to contact you if circumstances, including their own anxiety levels, change in any way before you are scheduled to respond.

Keep notes. You don't have to transcribe meetings word by word, but when people complain you should have some reasonably orderly system for noting the date, who was present, the gist of the information presented to you, and any action you promise. The longer you leave matters unrecorded, the more creative later renditions will become. Contemporaneous notes are much more useful than subsequent re-creations.

If a problem escalates and comes under scrutiny from an external agency or becomes the subject of a lawsuit, these notes may later have to be made public or given to others through freedom of information acts, laws permitting employees to inspect personnel records, or the discovery process associated with lawsuits. That possibility does not mean you shouldn't take and keep notes; it merely makes it all the more important that the notes be confined to fac-

tual matters. These notes are not the place to record stray judgments or editorial comments about the complaint or the people involved. An attorney representing a university in a sticky case once
told me about a department head's notes of a pivotal telephone call
that contained comments like "What a jerk!" and a drawing of a
firing squad. Do not put yourself in such a position.

Another form of note is useful as well: it's a good idea to send the
person with whom you met a short note—on paper or by email—
confirming that the meeting occurred and sketching out what was
said. It might read something like this: "Thank you for coming to
see me today. I found it useful to hear about your concerns. As I
said in our meeting, I will gather more information about this situation because I had no previous knowledge of it. I expect to get
back to you by next Thursday. If there is any change in this schedule, I'll notify you."

Trust your instincts if you are fearful. When you feel anxious about
dealing with a situation, pay attention to the feeling and call upon
someone from the appropriate university office for advice and/or
help. There are many kinds of discomfort and anxiety that attend
the handling of complaints: the general unpleasantness, not knowing what to expect, the hard conversations that may be involved—
the list is long. I'm not talking about a general disinclination to take
the next step or even dread of the coming meeting. What I'm talking about is being afraid, whether for your safety or for that of
someone else.

Fear is a visceral and primitive instinct. If you are afraid, trust the
instinct, and do not suppress it out of worry that your concerns
might be groundless. Sometimes fear stems from otherness or un-

predictability: the consultation I'm advising can help you differentiate that phenomenon from something far more serious to which you should be paying attention.

I once served as the hearing officer in a situation in which the grievant kept diverting his testimony to the multiple qualifications on different weapons that he had earned during his military service. After consulting with the university's police department and learning that the man had licenses for firearms, I made sure that every subsequent meeting took place in a building that had security screening at the entrances. It's not foolish to worry when someone talks to you about his attack dogs or is physically or verbally threatening. It's prudent. Troubled people sometimes cause harm to themselves or others. Don't take a chance.

Most academic institutions have people whose job is to deal with such problems, and who will be able to help you—but only if you call upon them. No one will think less of you for asking, and it is far better to be safe (even if you feel foolish) than to be sorry.

Some problems require formal process. There are some situations you should not try to handle informally or on your own. Virtually all formal personnel actions (reprimands, discipline, terminations, and so on) fall into this category. For those matters, seek advice from the professionals in your institution who have responsibility in the relevant area, whether they are lawyers, human resources staff, or other administrators. Beyond that, use formal process if the situation or problem has any of these characteristics:

- involves people who are extremely volatile,
- involves unusually large power differences—as when a student complains about the conduct of a star faculty member,

- has deep roots in the past (when people start to tell you about it, the first event they want to describe is five or ten years ago),
- involves allegations that, if true, are serious or possibly criminal, including the use of illegal substances, or
- involves sexual relationships.

For various reasons, situations like these are so complex and so fraught with possibilities for bad outcomes that you will benefit from the application—and the protection—of prescribed procedures. Soon after, or even before, beginning your new job, it's important to acquaint yourself with the rules and procedures, and to get acquainted with the resource people on your campus. Those helpful people may be in an employee assistance program, a human resources office, a counseling center, the dean's office, or the provost's office. Find out who they are and what they have to offer *before* you have a serious problem on your hands.

Take a witness with you. There are some circumstances in which you should not meet with a person one-on-one. When people are under stress, the presence of a third party can help keep the tone balanced and provide additional recollection of the conversation; even innocuous statements made in such circumstances have the potential to be mis- or over-interpreted. It pays to have a third participant at a meeting when emotions are running high, when you are delivering bad news, when the person with whom you are meeting is volatile, or when you have reason to think the person has selective hearing. If you've found, with a particular person, that saying "I can't make any promises, but I'll look into the situation" turns into "You promised to change that," then do not meet with that person alone again. If someone has a history of turning against those who have tried to help (for example, by filing charges against them), then don't meet with that person alone. Have a witness to what is actually said—and both you and your witness should take notes at the meeting or immediately afterward. Be careful whom you invite to be a witness. Confidentiality is important to consider as well as how the person complaining will perceive your choice. Another administrator is a good choice—a human resources professional, for example.

Retaliation Charges

Complaints of retaliation are the fastest-growing category of lawsuits against universities. Typically, even if a complaint is ultimately found to be without merit, the person who brought it may still sue, claiming that he or she was mistreated *as a result of* filing the complaint. This puts an extra burden on you to warn all participants in these situations that they *must not* have any interactions with the complainant while the complaint is pending or during the review or investigation process. This will run counter to what the accused person wants to do, which is to confront the accuser right away. Your job will be to make sure that no action that affects the status of the person bringing the complaint happens without legal review and blessings. This is much harder than it sounds, because not only will you have to review personnel or student actions—reassignment, termination, dismissal, discipline, or the like—that may have been under way before the complaint was filed (and that may well have triggered the complaint), but you may also have to calm down your department members and educate them about the danger of being drawn into the proceedings if the complainant perceives them to be making nasty comments, mean looks, and so on.

As with so many aspects of these problems, there are some fine lines: I recall a woman complaining that her co-workers were retaliating against her because they didn't invite her out to lunch with them after she filed discrimination charges against a popular supervisor whose disciplinary action against her had been widely supported. This was *not* retaliation: the other employees had the right to associate as they saw fit in their personal time (they were not paid for their lunch hour). But it could have been seen as retaliation if any of them had had supervisory responsibilities for the woman. It is absolutely essential that the person against whom the complaints are filed do *nothing* that could be seen as hostile or adverse to the person who complained. The more you can maintain the status quo regarding the complainant until the process is over, the better. If changes that affect that person must be made, make them only with legal advice.

Is Rehabilitation Possible?

If a review of someone's conduct yields a finding that rules have been broken, especially if the violations are serious, it is critical to assess the violator's attitude before deciding what action to take. Educational institutions should believe in the value of forgiveness and rehabilitation, but should apply that belief in a clear-sighted way. In many circumstances, you may feel an intuitive identification with the violator, especially if he or she is young, has much in common with you, or has received many years of advanced training. Your impulse will be to preserve the person's career, if possible.

As you consider your possible actions, keep in mind the dangers of false or misguided compassion. Of course it makes sense to give extra chances to the young, especially in an educational institution—but compassion is misguided when it shields people from the consequences of their own bad choices and bad behavior (especially when the bad behavior is repeated), or when it penalizes someone else. Granting an extra chance to a person with marginal qualifications or achievements is likely to leave a more qualified person without a seat in an educational program or a chance at a tenured position.

Misguided compassion is also likely to cost time and money. Remarkably often, a person who is granted an exception against good practice or good judgment will become a repeat customer. By the time you finally do draw the line with such a person, the problem will be much more difficult to handle than it would have been if you had applied the rules evenhandedly all along. Even worse, allowing exceptions to well-designed rules may, over time, make those rules unenforceable, and it may open the institution to claims that exceptions are granted arbitrarily or in a discriminatory fashion. If a rule is so harsh that those in authority are constantly seeking ways to avoid enforcing it, it is far better to reexamine and revise the rule than to apply it on an ad hoc basis.

Besides scrutinizing your own impulses, you must also consider four questions about the rule breaker's attitude before deciding how lenient or how punitive to be:

- Does the transgressor understand the offense? That is, does he understand what the rule means, why it exists, and why it matters that it was broken? Or is his response that the rule did not really matter, or that it only applied to others?
- Does the rule breaker accept responsibility? Or does she claim that her action was someone else's fault—that the secretary, the student, the colleagues, or the system imposed so many

pressures that the rule had to be broken? Without acceptance that she is responsible for her own conduct, rehabilitation cannot take place.

- Has the violator expressed remorse for breaking the rule, or taken any action to prevent recurrence or to apologize? Or is he mostly sorry he got caught?
- Has the wrongdoer taken any steps to make up for the wrong?

In American society, rehabilitation requires taking responsibility, feeling remorse, vowing to reform, and, where possible, offering recompense. Think of these as the "four R's." Thus it is important that the transgressor make a statement that is clear on all four of these grounds. It might be something like this:

> I made a serious mistake when I omitted data points from my report. I'm sorry I did that, and I am especially sorry that it caused so much trouble for the lab. I have learned not only that my notebook matters, but that communication with my colleagues and collaborators is also an important part of my work. I will follow your recommendations [specify these] for changing the way I work. I know I cost everyone a lot of time, and I will work over spring break to try to help us catch up.

Anything short of that kind of clear statement—especially if it includes components like "But others did the same thing" or "The lab was such a mess that I couldn't help it"—does not bode well, and in fact indicates that if you choose leniency you may be inviting recidivism. If a transgressor fails to accept responsibility, express remorse for violating a rule, or cooperate in offering recompense, a rehabilitation plan will be a waste of time. In that situation, the institution should consider imposing a meaningful penalty, with the goal of reinforcing its overall ethical environment. The message you send to department members should *not* be that crime does pay after all.

In all of these situations, think about what a university is trying to achieve from the perspective of its multiple constituencies. In its educational mission, it must do more than provide topic-specific instruction and training. Undergraduates care about the totality of their experience, especially on residential campuses, including being consistently treated with respect. Graduate education must give students the tools to undertake a complex transformation from being consumers of knowledge to becoming creators of knowledge. This requires personalized guidance throughout a student's time at the university. Faculty and professional employees don't just care about their paychecks but also seek interesting colleagues, good facilities, and intellectual stimulation. All employees care about fair and evenhanded treatment. External constituencies seek value for their investments in the university (whether through state allocations for public universities or through federal research funding for all universities), and they seek accountability. Alumni want to be proud of their home institution, not to read about its scandals in the newspaper. The list could go on. This multiplicity of constituencies means that it is worthwhile thinking in a very broad sense about what constitutes an ethical environment and how to meet those expectations.

The good news is that a little common sense goes a long way in dealing with problems, especially if you apply this chapter's tips and guidelines consistently. When you lapse, don't beat yourself up; accept that you goofed, and fix what can be fixed. Think of it this way: the job is hard because it's hard, not because you're defective. And as part of your new expertise at maintaining good boundaries, try not to take the problems home with you.

Professor Holdover's Teaching

So what can you do about Professor Holdover's ramblings and erratic behavior in the classroom? There are a number of issues and stakeholders to identify in this situation before you proceed. There are educational issues, questions of the academic freedom of a tenured faculty member, fairness, and complex matters of process and questions of the applicable policies.

The first order of business is to decide what to say to the students who have come to see you, as they are likely to press you for commitments or assurances before they leave your office. They will be concerned about retaliation if Holdover learns they are complaining, and they will also want to know what you will do about their grades in the course. While you can seek other sources of information about the problems in the course, it is likely that the professor will have to be told their names at some point in the process. You need to say something to prepare them for this eventuality; don't give them the impression that you'll keep their identities confidential. After you're sure you've heard all their concerns—using your best listening skills—you'll need our second key sentence, in which you tell them you need to talk with others before you can act. Give a time and date when you will meet with them again, and do your best to leave them feeling reassured that you'll be getting back to them. Among other things, you'd like to be sure they leave the matter in your hands for at least a short period before they start taking their complaints elsewhere.

You will want to confer with the undergraduate studies director—and fairly quickly, as in this situation you need to be ready to
meet with Professor Holdover as soon as possible. You may need to
consult with your campus contact for legal or human resources issues, as the students raised a possible issue of substance abuse or im-
pairment, which is one of the red flags for getting legal advice before acting.

Prepare in advance for your talk with Holdover, because you will
want to keep this first conversation focused on your agenda, and
not let it be deflected onto other topics, such as the students' shortcomings. What will your first sentence be? How will you open the
conversation? As soon as you mention that students have expressed
concerns, you are likely to encounter righteous indignation and a
demand to know exactly who is complaining. So, while that fact
needs to come into the conversation at a fairly early stage, it's a
good idea to work on rapport building for a few minutes at the beginning of the conversation. If you start by asking how the semester
is going, you may elicit helpful information. Maybe his conduct in
class was some kind of cry for help; maybe he'll tell you he's not
feeling well, or open the topic of his classroom behavior himself.
You'll be surprised what you can learn by listening before you talk.

If your opening does not elicit information, you will need to
have prepared your key sentence about the complaint, as well as
your response when he asks who is complaining. If you are willing
to provide the names (and have told the students you may do so),
give them to him and go on. If you'd rather not reveal the names at
this point, be prepared with the exact words of your refusal. Either
way, it will be up to you to ensure that the conversation does not
get hijacked by Holdover's outrage at how bad students are these
days or his determination to uphold standards of excellence in the
face of their (and/or your) mediocrity.

As part of your preparation, you will have ascertained what rights and options you have for observing his teaching (in some places observation without permission is a gross violation of the institutional culture) or otherwise gaining more direct information about what occurs in his classroom. It may be that your institution's rules on capricious grading will give you some leverage, if you confirm that he indeed administered a test on material that had not yet been covered in class. The particulars of what you can do may be dictated by local policies and procedures, but you must find some way of collecting information while respecting Professor Holdover's rights and protecting the education of the students. You should also be sensitive to the students' fear (and the real possibility) of retaliation, and warn Holdover not to act in any way that could be perceived as retaliatory toward his students.

In the real-life version of this case study, Professor Holdover's initial response was total denial: he didn't have a problem, the students did. The university where he taught had proscriptions against classroom observation of a tenured professor and policies that prevented any action against him in mid-semester without a hearing, which would have taken so long that the students' needs would not have been met. The head of the department and its executive committee, acting together, devised a novel solution. Since they couldn't observe his class directly (they changed their departmental policy on this matter in the following semester), a member of the executive committee volunteered to teach another section of the course. Students were informed that another section of the course had opened (without any indication of cause), and would meet at the same times as Holdover's section. Each student was offered the opportunity to transfer to the new section—and all of them did so. Only then did the professor acknowledge that he'd been having problems and agree to see his physician, who discovered that he had suffered a series of small strokes. The executive committee rounded up more faculty volunteers to offer tutoring sessions on the missed material, and Professor Holdover went on disability leave.

Sometimes you'll need to be creative in collecting information or devising solutions. But you'll always need to hear more than one version of the story and to be sure you're on firm procedural grounds before you act.

Chapter 5

Bullies

You are now the head of a large unit in which you have been a faculty member for many years. Until you became head, you were not fully aware of the problems with one of your colleagues, Professor Choler. Now you feel besieged by complaints from staff members about his treatment of them.

You remember, over the years, having received Choler's periodic email messages—sent to the whole department—complaining about one matter or another, but since most of them didn't affect you directly, you paid little attention. You also knew that Choler could be unpleasant at faculty meetings, but he didn't attend very often, and most of his complaints were ruled out of order.

Now, however, both the messages and the conduct at faculty meetings have become your business. In his typical email message, Choler describes a problem, personalizes the fault to a single individual, and recommends a solution that usually involves humiliation, if not discipline, for that person. The people he targets (or, in some cases, their union representatives) are the ones complaining to you and demanding that you take action. In addition, a few faculty members have asked you to "get this email thing under control" because they don't want to be bothered by any more of his messages.

At meetings Choler uses the same general tactic, usually going after a particular person with strong language and in a loud voice. This makes some people so uncomfortable that they will not attend a meeting if they see him in the room. His victims have been known to leave meetings shaking, or even in tears, after his verbal assaults.

Reviewing the collection of email messages, plus other letters Choler sent to your predecessor, you have noticed a pattern to the situations. Generally he identifies a real problem. For example, his complaint about cumbersome and slow processing of travel vouchers was accurate, but his assignment of blame to a clerk in the business office was not, and his subsequent near-persecution of the clerk was (in your opinion, and certainly according to the clerk and her union steward) disproportionate to the problem and to her role in processing vouchers. Once Choler picks a target, he rarely lets up until that person leaves the department.

There is no evidence in the files that anyone has ever spoken to Professor Choler about his email tirades or his conduct in meetings.

Have you ever had a guest with an uncontrolled child or pet? The most intractable problems in academia have the same characteristics: someone running loose in your environment who does not stay within prevailing concepts of acceptable behavior. I'm not talking about behavior that is merely unusual or eccentric; in a university, especially, odd is okay if your work gets done and you don't interfere with the ability of others to do theirs. I'm talking about someone whose refusal to play by the generally accepted rules causes trouble for the rest of your department. If you have not encountered this kind of troublemaker, use what follows as a form of inoculation against any such problems that might later infect your unit.

Some difficult people are merely minor irritants: others learn to avoid them as much as possible, and the overall working environment is not badly compromised. But a person who targets others, makes threats (direct or indirect), insists on his or her own way all the time, or has such a hair-trigger temper that colleagues walk on eggshells to avoid setting it off, can paralyze a department. In the worst cases, this conduct can create massive dysfunction as the department finds itself unable to hold meetings, make hiring decisions, recruit new members, or retain valued ones.

When I first got involved in helping department heads cope with such people, my colleagues and I used concepts and approaches we gleaned from studies of bullies. When we started, the literature was largely restricted to bullies among children, and the most useful concepts we found were related to bully-proofing elementary schools. In the years since then, many books have appeared about adult bullies, including those in the workplace, but these works have not brought about any major changes in the approach we refined using our own experience and the concepts we found in our original explorations of research focused on children.

The bullies I have encountered—and helped to neutralize—in the academic environment come in many forms, from those who present themselves as victims ("You violated my rights and I'm entitled to special treatment to make up for it") all the way to classic aggressors who rely on physical intimidation. In academia and other settings populated by "knowledge workers," one often encounters other kinds of bullies as well, including "memo bullies" (who send regular missives to a long mailing list) and "insult bullies" (destructive verbal aggressors).

Characteristics of Bullies

Whatever their approaches, bullies are people who are willing to cross the boundaries of civilized behavior that inhibit others. They value the rewards brought by aggression and generally lack guilt, believing their victims provoked the attacks and deserve the consequences. Their behavior prompts others to avoid them, which means that, in the workplace, bullies are likely to become effectively unsupervised. If you think about the constellation of qualities that characterize bullying behavior, and especially the effects of that behavior in an environment that prizes collegiality and independence, and in which many members are conflict-averse, it's not hard to see why many people tend to withdraw instead of dealing with the bullies.

Remember the earlier discussion about stars? Sometimes your stars will have bullying characteristics, but more often the most problematic bullies are not major stars in your unit. They're simply people who have frequently gotten what they wanted through their outrageous conduct—and have even been rewarded in various ways for that conduct. If your bully is, in fact, a star whom it would be costly to lose, you'll need to proceed with extra caution, but it's your job to think about the good of the community as a whole: even stars must not be allowed to cause fear or impede the productivity of others.

In the worst case of an unsupervised bully I ever saw, a worker in a university's physical plant who had a habit of making direct threats ("I have guns hidden all over the campus") was assigned a job with no set hours, no duties for which he was held accountable—and the use of a university truck that he took home every night. His supervisors were (understandably) afraid of him, and they didn't want to take the risk that he would turn on them. It took a concerted team effort over many months (and a transfer to a different unit with different supervisors through two levels of responsibility) to bring this man back into a situation where he was actually performing work in exchange for his paycheck. (It didn't last long, though. He was arrested after an incident in his personal life, and took up residence as a guest of the state.) Across all categories of employment, bullies become unsupervised: I've seen secretaries, faculty members, and businesspeople who were so unpleasant to deal with that they were neither given the same duties as others in their environment nor held accountable for the duties they did hold.

My colleague Dr. Paul Joffe, a clinical psychologist who facilitated many of our workplace problem-solving teams, did much of the early literature review and brought the concepts about bullies to our working group. One of the major insights he brought us is that there are two major types of bullies: aggressor bullies and victim bullies. Aggressor bullies fit the usual idea of a bully: they threaten to beat you up if you don't give them your lunch money. Victim bullies, in contrast, demand your lunch money because of some harm they claim you've done to them. Think of someone running into you in the schoolyard, then asserting that you should give him your lunch money because you knocked him down and made him tear his pants. That's a classic victim bully. In workplaces, victim bullies are aggrieved and are trying to get their own way as recompense for their perceived mistreatment. Most of the bullies I have encountered in academia have been victim bullies, not aggressor bullies.

While many workplaces have bullies, institutions of higher education may be especially vulnerable to them because of some of the distinctive characteristics of academia. First, bullies flourish in the decentralized structure of universities: the isolation of so many microclimates, from laboratories to small departments, creates many opportunities for a bully to run roughshod over colleagues. Then too, the bullies of academia typically manipulate the concepts of academic freedom and collegiality with flair, and their colleagues are not well equipped, and not trained, to respond to their maneuvers. The propensity of bullies to misuse these central academic concepts only adds to the importance of being well grounded in those concepts yourself. If you have a firm understanding of what academic freedom is and what it is not, you'll be better prepared to cope with those who try to distort the concept for their own ends.

Another reason people in academia are generally unprepared to deal with bullies is that bullies are relatively rare. It's worth thinking about what are known as "low-incidence, high-severity" problems. This concept can be applied to a variety of situations that arise in academic settings, especially in personnel matters. A low-incidence, high-severity situation is one in which the problems don't arise very often, but when they do they are so serious that they can threaten the integrity of the environment. Bullying falls into this category. Research misconduct also falls into this category, and so do other serious violations of laws and regulations (see Chapter 7).

For these infrequent but major problems, it makes sense to focus on preventive and educational efforts rather than waiting to cope with the problem each time it arises. For research misconduct, that means ensuring that there is plenty of discussion about positive standards and expectations, as well as information and assistance for those encountering ethical dilemmas. Just as we do not expect students to acquire their substantive expertise by osmosis or mind-reading, we should not ask them to absorb professional ethics without direct formal and informal instruction. For prevention of bullying, creating and maintaining an environment in which respectful professional interactions are expected and reinforced is the most powerful approach.

When unprofessional or uncivil conduct occurs in the workplace, it's important to nip it in the bud. The tone of your response should be nonconfrontational: "Oh, I'm sorry, maybe we forgot to tell you that we don't act that way here." Dealing with the problem head-on and promptly is critical.

Before taking action against a person accused of violating the rules, you will of course investigate the charges. If your investigation substantiates them, it is essential that you impose sanctions. If someone is verbally abusive to staff or threatens physical violence, the appropriate penalty must be imposed. Otherwise, you send the message that the conduct in question is acceptable.

If those responsible for supervising problematic employees hesitate to ask legitimate questions within the scope of their duties ("Do you have the required receipts for this expenditure?") for fear of triggering temper tantrums, a person of higher authority should be brought in to enforce the regulations. Any other response—such as simply accepting the behavior or slinking away in the face of the histrionics—only erodes the trust of those who work hard to do the right thing. Similarly, ignoring or tolerating inappropriate conduct in the workplace sends the message to all those who do behave professionally that the way to prosper is to misbehave, not to follow the rules.

How to Handle a Bully

I once got a request from a department administrator (let's call him Barry Holmes) for advice about how to deal with a visiting faculty member (and let's call him Raymond Cooper) whose contract was to expire in just a few weeks. Cooper had been verbally explosive all year, so people had learned to tread gently around him. But recently his volatility had increased, and a colleague who collaborated with him on research had begun to feel unsafe around him, fearing that his verbal aggression might become physical. Holmes wanted to know what he could do—if anything—to get to the end of the semester safely.

I asked Holmes how he had responded to Cooper's earlier explosions. He had done nothing. This was better news than I had expected, as I'm often told something like "Well, that's just the way he is, so we've tried to give him what he wants and not make him mad." Nevertheless, the hands-off approach was not going to solve the problem.

Avoidance Is Not Effective

Avoidance is one of the basic responses to conflict (others include denial, appeasement, negotiation, mediation, and "because I say so"), and it can be a wise response, especially when the issues are relatively small, of fleeting duration, and of little lasting consequence. Avoiding engagement with an issue is a positive reaction to someone's momentary venting when you're pretty sure the issue will pass. It's a particularly good strategy at the end of the semester during the "silly season," when everyone is under stress. But avoidance is hardly ever the right response when a person has shown a pattern of threatening or escalating conduct or when an important principle is at stake.

On the topic of the visiting Professor Cooper, I asked the department head whether and how Cooper had been informed that his outbursts were causing concern. Well, Holmes responded, "everybody knows" that that kind of behavior is unprofessional. I advised calling Cooper in, nonetheless, and telling him that his conduct was unsettling to his colleagues and students. I reminded Holmes that mind-reading is an imperfect form of communication, and that he'd be doing both Cooper and the intimidated collaborator a favor by letting Cooper know—unequivocally—that he was expected to control his behavior and to conduct himself professionally in all interactions with colleagues, students, and staff. People who are acting out need to be told clearly that there will be consequences for uncivil behavior. Otherwise, they'll have little incentive to exercise self-control.

Holmes acknowledged that this made sense. But what could he say, and how should he say it? Academics seem to find it particularly difficult to raise troublesome topics, especially ones involving the personal conduct of a colleague. Over the years I've learned to recommend a three-step process: First, try to identify and describe a pattern in what you're observing. In this case, the escalating explosive verbal conduct is the pattern, and it intimidates others. It sounds like a bullying situation. Second, sketch out a general strategy. In this case, the strategy is to send the message to the offender that this sort of behavior is not welcome in this department or this university. Finally, it is tremendously helpful to outline the points you wish to communicate and practice how you'll say them. Having identified the pattern of the problem and chosen a strategy, Holmes and I discussed the points he should cover in a conversation with Cooper and possible ways to phrase them. In particular, we rehearsed his opening lines and worked to put the concepts into his own voice, to find words and approaches he could make his own.

Let's say you are in Holmes's position: the department head faced with the volatile Cooper. The points to make in your talk with Cooper are, first, that his behavior is disturbing to others; second, that you are serious about maintaining a nonviolent work and learning environment; and finally, that you refer all threats and acts of violence to the campus police. (Some universities have official written policies that can be used to reinforce that last point.) You can tell Cooper, calmly and clearly, that you have learned from various students and staff members that he has seemed increasingly frustrated and has often been heard shouting. You can then express a sincere desire to be able to write a positive recommendation for him in his search for his next position. Be sure your words convey the message that you expect him to change his behavior—a warning that he is approaching, and has crossed at times, a boundary that must *not* be crossed.

After the conversation, you should send a cordial and factual confirming letter restating the gist of what was said. Some people's eyes work better than their ears, and you want to be sure Cooper gets your message. The letter should be short and sweet and say something like this:

Dear Ray:

Thank you for taking the time to talk with me this morning. I appreciated your responsiveness in our conversation about effective ways to work in our department. As I said, I have been told that you seem increasingly frustrated and that recently you have been heard shouting on a number of occasions. While we all encounter frustrations, the frequency and level of your expression have been disturbing other members of the department. We expect everyone in our unit to contribute to a collegial and professional atmosphere. Thank you for your contributions, both professional and educational.

Cordially,

[your signature]

After the conversation and the confirming letter, let's hope no further action will be necessary. If, however, Cooper's conduct does not revert to the upsetting-but-tolerable category until his departure, your next response will be to call the campus police, who will supply a bit of what my colleagues and I have come to call "blue therapy," involving a talk with a uniformed (and trained) peace officer. On the basis of past experience, I predict that, should the need arise, the interaction with the police will be both educational for Cooper and therapeutic for his tantrum habit.

This problem is relatively straightforward and amenable to correction because it is of recent origin—at least in your department—and because you have more leverage over a visitor than over one of your tenured faculty members. Since Cooper is about to move on to another short-term position, apparently making a career out of visiting, your recommendation, or your opinion of him as relayed by word of mouth, is likely to matter. The chances are quite high that he has a history of similar behavior at other places, and he may have found that many institutions don't check references when hiring or that most of the places he's worked in the past won't mention this conduct, even if asked for a reference. Letting him know that you take references seriously may well have an impact. Then again, it's possible that, precisely because he is a short-termer, he won't bother to adapt his behavior. In that case, "blue therapy" is likely to be the most effective response, and it will have the side benefit of showing other department members that there are definite consequences for out-of-bounds conduct.

In contrast to this problem, many situations involving academic bullies date back years, if not decades. Problems with long histories are not quickly resolved. In fact, it generally takes more than a year to bring about significant change in a pattern of conduct that stretches back over years. But the key point to hold in mind is that significant, positive change can be achieved, given the right mind-set, some patience, and persistence.

Change the Environment

The key to changing a bully's behavior is to change the environment. Think back to the advice in Chapter 1, about the basic mind-set to bring to leadership positions. Most people want to be liked, to be successful, and to be respected in their profession. Even bullies have these characteristics in the main, and many of them have not been made consciously aware of the destructive effects of their actions. Of course, some people are quite calculating about getting their way through their conduct, and we'll talk more about them later. But for bullies across the spectrum, most have never been confronted with the consequences of their actions, or even been told that their conduct is not well regarded in their environment. Why? For the reasons discussed earlier: others in the environment are conflict-averse; it doesn't feel "nice" or collegial to raise the issue; co-workers have learned to avoid any behavior likely to trigger the bully's temper. Thus your task is to change the environment to begin attaching natural consequences to unpleasant behavior, and most of all, to remove any rewards it has yielded. This is the essence of the hard work to come.

Think of it as changing the parent's response to the child's grocery store tantrum from a candy bar to some signal of disapproval. The form this disapproval takes can vary, and it takes conscious thought, planning, and some coalition building. In the early stages, especially, making the changes can involve inconvenience to others: one of the steps a parent may need to take in combating the temper tantrum in public is to leave the public setting, even if that means the shopping is left undone. But any parent who has faced out even one such public event knows the salutary effect of holding the line. Don't cave in.

Let's say you have a faculty member who is abusive to the department's secretaries. He brings them typing at the last minute and expects it to be done right away, regardless of their other duties. He insists that his work get priority and generally is unpleasant enough that one of the secretaries either moves his work up in the queue or stays late to do it. His approach has always gotten him what he wants, and both the secretaries and the faculty members whose work gets delayed are unhappy and are complaining to you.

The first step will be to *tell* him that his conduct with the secretaries is upsetting and is not appropriate. You will need to provide guidance about proper protocols for interactions and establish guidelines for reasonable work turn-around periods. Count on him to test your commitment to your stated position: the most likely response is that he will call you on the new deadlines by submitting something late in which you have a stake (like a grant application) to force you to choose whether to enforce your rule or back down.

If you can anticipate this eventuality and put up safeguards against it first—charging his funds for extra help to free up departmental staff to meet his deadline, for example—you'll be ahead of the game.

Alternatively, you could change the way he is permitted to use the resource the secretaries represent: you could assign one point of entry for his support requirements, such as bringing his work to you (in a small department) or to a senior staff member with a robust personality. Again, anticipate that his first level of response will be to test how serious you are. You should only choose new rules you can and will stand behind, and you should be prepared to take some inconvenience or pain as a likely consequence of standing firm.

While the goal is to make changes in the environment that remove the positive reinforcement the bully has been receiving for his or her actions, don't try to change too many factors too fast, especially in a situation where the bully has been holding sway for years. The corrective changes involve moving the boundaries closer to the acceptable range incrementally and gradually. So don't try to change everything at once: focus on what really matters. Is it the shouting, the insistence on having his work done before others', or the last-minute nature of the demands? Pick one and start trying to change it. Stick with it until you achieve your goal.

If Not You, Who?

All this sounds like a lot of work, and you may be asking yourself why you should bother. Especially if your term as chair or head is relatively brief—say a three-year rotation—and you'll soon go back to the faculty, why should you take the trouble to make the bully a more constructive part of the department? Why not just find coping mechanisms and live with the situation? You could do that. Many people do. In fact, if you have an entrenched problem of some duration, it's pretty much guaranteed that your predecessors took this route. So why not continue that tradition? Life is pretty short to buy trouble, after all.

Before you decide, there are two important things to consider. The first is that it's not hopeless—you can make a difference. True, taking action will not be without cost. That brings us to the second point. What will be the costs of inaction? After all, it's not just your personal discomfort or safety that's at issue.

How many victims—direct or indirect—in your environment are suffering from the bully's behavior? Direct victims are easy to see: they're the ones who get up and run out of meetings (or don't attend in the first place), the ones who bear the brunt of the bully's attacks and insults. In your calculus about whether to act, they're probably already included, and perhaps you've thought of ways to make it easier on them.

But what of the indirect victims? What are your students, for example, learning about how faculty members behave? What is happening to the junior faculty, or to the staff members: are they afraid to speak up or participate fully in the life of the department? Who may have good ideas but doesn't dare to express them? Are there people you expected to make contributions, or to succeed, who are not doing so? Is this because of some failure on their part, or is there perhaps something about the environment that is impeding their success?

Look around and see what the untenured members of your department are enduring and what they're learning about how established professionals in your field treat one another. Is this the message you want them to absorb and then potentially pass along as they mature in their careers? Think about it: ignoring inappropriate conduct in your professional environment has long-term negative consequences.

It takes more than one person to change an environment. While someone must take responsibility for articulating the positive norms of the group, the most successful approaches involve a small but critical mass of colleagues (say three or four people) who are prepared to react in reasonably consistent ways to conduct that breaches those norms. The idea is to ensure that there is a response to each and every instance of behavior that violates the articulated norms, even if it is as low-key as merely labeling the behavior as troubling.

When I was in high school and enmeshed in the politics of a clique of girls, a particularly mature member of the group had a knack for defusing cattiness by quietly saying "That hurt my feelings. I feel really bad now." She didn't make these observations accusingly or with anger, but as simple declarations. I still remember my amazement at her ability to be so real in the moment, and also at the apologies she triggered. Genuine responses to nastiness are powerful. Suppose your group interactions tend to clever put-downs, but your bully pushes the boundaries and is venomous where others are good-natured. If the target or anyone else in the group responds, in the pleasant tones the group normally uses, "Ouch, that one really hurt," or even "That's not nice!" the painful comment is marked as beyond accepted boundaries. Don't follow the comment with hectoring or accusations, but instead let it stand on its own. Noting each over-the-line remark in this low-key fashion can be remarkably effective. It moves the group from shared, unspoken discomfort to modeling a socially acceptable response.

A stronger stance may be called for when the verbal bullying occurs in a more formal setting. Especially if you're presiding, it's important that you not permit personal attacks to occur in the guise of department business. Immediately ruling the remarks out of order and inviting the speaker to rephrase them to focus on the substance, not the person, is appropriate. Aside from the discomfort of the confrontation, you do risk turning yourself into the bully's target when you do this. This is where coalition-building comes into play, and where it's vital to be firmly within the group's accepted boundaries when you respond. Don't overreact or make yourself the problem: be sure your comment is quiet but firm and phrased politely.

Making such changes can be daunting. It takes advance planning and practice. The most critical ingredient is a calm and assertive approach that is neither punitive nor aggressive. The reality is that bullies—people who value the rewards brought by aggression—have a higher tolerance for conflict than the rest of us, and are likely to respond to signs of aggression by escalating their own aggressive behavior. Their escalation will rapidly surpass the coping abilities of even fairly strong individuals. As a result, staying positive, calm, and clear is central to succeeding in these situations.

What If the Bully Is Your Boss?

Dealing with bullying behavior within your department is difficult enough, but it's even harder to cope when the bullying is done by someone with supervisory authority over you. Unfortunately, there are no easy solutions to this problem, which comes up disturbingly often.

First you need a careful diagnosis of the patterns of conduct you're seeing, their seriousness, and how many people they are affecting. If what you perceive as inappropriate or unprofessional bullying is directed primarily or solely at you, and it's severe, not something you can grin and bear, your best bet is probably to cut your losses and leave. If you're isolated in that kind of situation, unless the bully is very near the end of his or her career, the costs to you from staying are likely to be vastly disproportionate to the benefits, no matter how strong your commitment to the institution. This is especially the case if your bête noir is relatively recently appointed and basking in official favor.

If the problem is more widely shared and/or acknowledged, you still must exercise great care and caution, and should still consider whether you'd be better off leaving. The nature of authority in organizations means that you're facing an uphill battle in which you may well come to be seen as the problem. There are constructive steps that can be taken, but they are far beyond the scope of this book and require an ongoing delicate calculus, the essence of which, at every turn, must be whether it's more costly to you to persevere than to move on.

Responding to Professor Choler

The most striking thing about Professor Choler's behavior is his consistent arrogation of authority to himself that belongs to others. Not only does he point out problems in the performance of others who do not have a reporting relationship to him (that is, for whom he is not a part of the evaluation or supervisory chain), but he takes it upon himself to "punish" them.

To change the environment so as to affect his conduct, you will need to reclaim your authority as the head of the department, and you will need to draw boundaries around his ability to affect the working condition of others so detrimentally. Steps to take before talking directly with him depend upon the structure of your institution and department, but it might be a good idea to have discussions with your dean and your executive committee to clarify lines of responsibility. This could provide a good foundation for what you will need to do next. It might even be useful to raise the issue in a faculty or department meeting, perhaps framed as a review of departmental operating policies.

Once you've affirmed that your authority over the members of the department (and especially the support staff) is generally acknowledged, it's time to have a face-to-face conversation with Professor Choler. Since part of your agenda is to reclaim your authority, it's important for this meeting to take place in your office, at your request. You should consider in advance whether to limit the discussion to a single topic—a stronger show of authority on your part—or whether you wish to cover other topics as well. Some of this will depend upon your own comfort level and upon other circumstances in the department. Have you already met with all faculty members individually (in their offices), for example? Are you familiar with Choler's ongoing work and professional situation? Do you have other business pending with him? It's worth thinking through these items before you begin. In general, your message will be conveyed more strongly if his interaction with the staff is the only topic of the meeting than if other items are also covered. Other topics may be useful, though, if your sense is that, with Choler, the best way to approach your main topic will be to lead up to it slowly and gradually.

Take one more step before the meeting: review Choler's emails and identify his rhetorical patterns; pick out several themes or words he uses repeatedly. Think about ways to frame your message in which you can employ those words in a positive way. Echo his own favorite phrases back to him.

Let's assume that "efficiency" and "effective" are words that recur in his missives. When you meet, start with the positive aspects of his actions: he is perceptive, he is committed to efficiency, and he seeks to improve the way your department works. These are praiseworthy traits. You might mention the example of the cumbersome voucher-processing system, and in discussing it, convey your expectation as head that in the future, when he notices such a problem, he will bring his complaint to you (or to someone else you designate). You should emphasize that, as head, you are responsible for the smooth and efficient functioning of the department, and that includes seeing that staff members perform their work properly. In a calm and clear way, you need to convey the dual message that he should bring problems to you and that it is not his place to chastise staff who do not report to him. The billing clerk, for example, reports to your business manager, and if Choler has a complaint about her performance, he should bring it to you—not to the clerk, and not to the faculty in meetings or by email—and you will take it up with her and her supervisor. You can emphasize your shared commitment to efficient functioning. You may want to point out that you are interested in his professional success, and you wish to relieve him of the burden of worrying about these matters (quite an inefficient use of his skills and time), so he can concentrate on his research and teaching.

Follow up the meeting with a short and cordial email (two or three sentences) thanking him for taking the time to talk with you and reiterating your commitment to addressing the concerns of members of the department and your expectation that, should he encounter a problem, he will bring it to you (or to the person you've designated). Copy yourself. Print out the message. Save it.

As to Choler's disruptive conduct in meetings, the first step will be to begin to articulate the group norm that interactions should be civil and collegial. It is always useful, when a meeting goes smoothly, or when a contentious matter is resolved professionally, to note that and to label it: "I've always liked the way our faculty resolves difficult problems without personalizing them." This kind of comment will both articulate the norm and provide a foundation for your later action. Start laying the groundwork at the first meeting over which you preside. Have a private conversation with each person who complains to you, in which you state that you will be responsible for running meetings, but that each member of the department must contribute both by being personally responsible and by supporting civil and collegial interactions.

If Choler's outbursts happen at every meeting, the process of changing the environment to change his behavior may require several discussions about how faculty meetings should operate, and may even require amending the department's bylaws to specify how topics get placed on the agenda. If he doesn't come to that many meetings, and if there is a consensus among those who do attend regularly that his conduct is out of bounds, start even if he is absent, and start early. Describe your interest in constructive and efficient meetings, and thus how you plan to run them, elicit suggestions (you may want to start your coalition building by raising the topic ahead of time in individual conversations with key faculty members), and be sure the minutes mention the discussion explicitly: "Procedures for departmental meetings and the role of the presiding officer were discussed." If your department has not distributed minutes in the past, start doing so now.

The next time Choler starts an attack during a meeting, interrupt him in a firm, positive, and polite tone: "Charlie, it's important that we be efficient in our meetings, and focus on issues, not personalities. Could you rephrase your comments so that we talk about the process issue? As you know, if you have a personnel matter to discuss, you and I can talk about it privately after the meeting."

Be persistent, positive, and above all, calm. Each time he begins one of his verbal assaults, smile and either reframe it and direct the discussion yourself, or place it on a future agenda for discussion. If he raises a concern that is shared by others, think about appointing a subcommittee to examine it, or assigning a staff member to look into it. Do not let a personal attack occur. If Choler doesn't respond to your calm intervention, you might suggest that he walk around the block to regain his composure. If someone else will chime in, with a friendly and positive (or humorous) tone, all the better. But don't sit by while a member of your department is personally attacked. If all else fails, adjourn the meeting. Try not to let the meeting turn into an escalating confrontation: use deflection techniques and humor, if you can, to focus on the issue, and to depersonalize the discussion as much as possible. The chances are very high that, especially if you have the support of the majority of those present, Professor Choler will back down and cooperate. The will of the majority can be a powerful force, even for someone who enjoys conflict. Everyone in the department will be reassured if you are fair and firm and focused on the issues—and if they see that you will not permit personal attacks.

Chapter 6

When Not to Improvise

You receive an anonymous letter reporting that Professor McNabb, a member of your department now on sabbatical at University A, has a full-time, paid faculty appointment there and is teaching courses. The letter also says that on her last sabbatical, eight years ago, McNabb received full pay for the entire academic year from University B, and that she taught courses there as well.

Your publicly supported university allows faculty members to augment their sabbatical pay only with grant and award support; it permits exceptions for honoraria for "a limited number of professional presentations" provided that they are approved in advance. The members of your Board of Regents are drawn from business and political sectors. In recent years they have repeatedly questioned the sabbatical system and sought extensive information about this perquisite for your faculty. The administration has prepared a number of reports showcasing advances in research and teaching made possible by sabbaticals and has increased the information provided to the Board with the annual requests for approval of sabbatical leaves. Nonetheless, this remains an area of tension between the administration and the Board. Several members of the state legislature's higher education committee also ask for information on faculty sabbaticals every few years.

Paperwork on file shows that McNabb received approval for a full-year sabbatical at full support (two-thirds pay). Her proposal describes a plan to collaborate with researchers at a specialized institute at University A in order to learn a new research technique. The plan approved for the previous sabbatical (also for a full year at two-thirds pay) was to visit a think tank affiliated with University B. The required report submitted after that sabbatical describes her research but does not mention any teaching.

When you consult with the dean, he says that Professor McNabb is probably the most important intellectual asset of your department, and that she often gets job offers from other institutions. He suggests that University A is using the sabbatical visit to recruit her, and urges you not to do anything that would upset or antagonize her.

There are some issues you just can't deal with on your own. Even if you have become totally comfortable in your administrative role, even if you have read and understand the nuances of all university policies that apply to your department—and even if you have a law degree—when issues with legal ramifications come across your desk, you need to consult with your institution's lawyers. (Depending on the prevailing culture, you may need to notify others, such as your dean, before calling the lawyers, especially if the lawyers are not on staff and are charging by the hour.)

Avoiding Lawsuits

"My dad (mom, uncle, grandfather, neighbor) is a lawyer and will be calling you (if you don't change my grade, give me a raise, make him stop it)." In twenty-first-century America, who doesn't worry about getting sued? Who isn't a little fearful of the time, money, and hassle that becoming embroiled in a lawsuit can involve? And, in higher education, who isn't a bit irritated at intrusions into academic matters by outsiders who invoke legality but care little about the values and mission of our institutions?

However we feel about it, though, we are entangled with the legal system and likely to stay that way. What does the savvy and survival-minded department head need to do to stay un-sued? The first thing to know is that, while common sense and a few rules you will learn in this chapter will go a long way, sometimes being sued is simply the price of being in business. I hasten to add: not very often. But the reality has to be faced: there are times when taking the correct institutional action means there is going to be a lawsuit. As any lawyer will tell you, the question is not "Can I get sued for this?" but instead "Can they win if they sue me for this?" Practically anyone can sue you for practically anything. The good news is that most lawsuits will go away long before they get to trial or judgment. Some will go away because they're meritless and some because your insurers are pusillanimous (they will call this businesslike) and pay off the "nuisance" claims because it costs less to buy closure than to defend and win. But most of them will go away. The question, of course, is how much they will cost you in time, psychic wear and tear, sleeplessness, or other unpleasantness before they disappear. And will they cost you money?

Luckily, as with so many aspects of an administrator's job, being properly prepared will help. There are some guidelines that will help you keep the situation from arising in the first place. That's what this chapter is about.

The first rule you need to know—and to follow, no matter what—is the one you've already heard in this chapter: Do not try to handle legal matters by yourself. The definition of a legal matter is any time you are contacted by a lawyer, or receive a legal document, or deal with an issue involving legal consequences. If you get a telephone call from a lawyer, do not discuss anything substantive without first getting advice from your institution's legal counsel. If you receive a legal document—even one that looks straightforward to you, such as a request for information about the monthly salary of someone who owes child support or a request for a document you have in your files and think is innocuous—do not provide the document or the information without first talking to your institution's legal staff.

This simple rule will help you. No matter how smart, savvy, and experienced you are, it is not your job to be the lawyer. Do not guess or assume you know the best way to respond to an outside lawyer. Get advice. And follow it. Even if you have heard through the grapevine that your university's lawyers are second-rate, the likelihood that the institution will cover any legal bills you incur is much better if the lawyers are involved from the beginning of every matter. And there are some counterintuitive things that happen in the legal world that they should be able to protect you from—if and only if you consult them.

I recall a department head who knew this rule but ignored it when a member of his staff was involved in a child-custody case. The staff member's lawyer asked him to provide information to help her case. Everyone in the department liked the woman and knew what a creep her ex-husband was. The department head's well-meaning action eventually cost him several days of his time, as the opposing lawyer called him for a deposition in the case. He found the experience deeply distasteful: under oath, he was asked many questions about his own personal life as well as that of the staff member. Evidently the lawyer was fishing for evidence that the department head and the staff member had any "personal" (a euphemism) relationship. They didn't, but the questions were intrusive and offensive. Many he didn't have to answer, but the fact that they were posed at all made the deposition an aversive experience.

The time and effort of preparing for the deposition (including collecting more documents than he had known the university held about the staff member and himself) and then enduring it could probably have been saved if the department head had simply referred the original request to the office of the university counsel. The university's lawyers have a set procedure for verifying and responding to such requests, and their participation insulates supervisors from personal involvement in such matters. To his credit, the department head used his sad experience to warn his colleagues against dealing with legal matters without consulting the counsel's office. Wherever he could, he advised other department heads to heed the advice on this point offered at the administrative orientation session. He spread the word far and wide—but attention spans are short and memory attenuates. Not thirteen months later, the head of another department responded in almost precisely the same way, with the same results, because it was the same lawyer, who had added the technique to his arsenal.

So, rule number one is: Don't play lawyer, even for seemingly routine or minor matters, and even if you have a law degree or know a lot about the legal system. Let the institution's lawyers—who are paid to do this—represent you in legal matters.

Now for rule number two: Learn the institutional policies that govern your actions as a department head in each of the following areas:

- hiring
- evaluation
- remediation/firing
- discrimination/harassment, including ADA (disability accommodations)
- compliance issues (research misconduct, protection of human and animal research subjects, grants policies, family leave act, personnel and student privacy issues, and so on).

In each of these areas, you must know, in advance, the limits upon your range of action, the specific policies that apply, what you are expected to do and when, and the resource people you can consult at your institution. For example, as the leader of the department, are you responsible for ensuring that every staff member is evaluated once a year? Once every three years? Are you expected to sign off on these evaluations? Are you expected to certify to a central office that the required evaluations have been completed? Who sets the standards against which staff are to be evaluated? Are the standards different for different categories of employees? If people in the department think the standards are being applied more strictly for some than for others, are you the one who'll be sued for discrimination? (Probably.) If a staff member in your department is to be terminated, does the firing occur in your name? If so, it pays to be sure that the evaluation process is fair and appropriate.

Are you beginning to get a feel for this? The rule of thumb in

America these days seems to be "Sue everyone." Thus, if you are the department head, and you are nominally or in fact responsible for a set of procedures, you are likely to be named in any lawsuit that results from unresolved problems. Since that's the case, you may as well accept that this is the reality and ensure that your house is in order from the very start. This is a responsibility that comes with your role.

Beyond the two basic rules—don't play lawyer, and learn your policies—here are some other important points to keep in mind when situations arise that might have legal implications.

Process and procedure are your friends. Process is especially vital in personnel and student-related matters. No matter how eager you are to resolve a problem quickly, your resolution will stick only if you scrupulously follow every appropriate procedural step. You can take immediate, decisive action and quite probably see it overturned, or you can painstakingly document every step in what may seem like an endless process—and see your resolution stand in the end.

Perceptions of power matter. People like and identify with underdogs. Whether or not you feel like an authority figure, you will be seen as the more powerful actor in any interaction with a student or a member of your department. If you act in ways that people may perceive (even if through misunderstanding) as high-handed or as abusing the power of your position, you will lose support. And you may lose more than that.

Focus on conduct, not motive. No matter how much insight you may think you have into what is motivating a person's behavior— family conflicts, general level of stress, stage in life, health or general stability—your role is *not* to share your insights or your diagnosis. Your role is solely related to setting and enforcing expectations for appropriate conduct in the environment for which you are responsible. Just as this means you should not say "You're being paranoid, Sam—everyone knows you get that way when the moon is full," it also means you should say something like this: "Sam, I am committed to providing a fair hearing to everyone in the department. If you believe something unjust has occurred, please tell me what happened, and I'll look into it. Meanwhile, my expectation is that you will follow our established procedures. It isn't appropriate to try to record advisory committee meetings without the knowledge or consent of the other people in the room."

Less is more in a dispute. When you're developing your written confirmation of a hard conversation (remember this good practice you've learned?), after you finish your first draft, go back through it and excise every adjective. Better yet, leave out any description of your feelings altogether. No one needs to know that you are disappointed or concerned, shocked, outraged, or appalled. This isn't about you. Stick to low-key, factual statements. Go for understatement. Records accumulate over time, and the sheer aggregation will begin to matter. More than that, think of the "third reader." That's the outsider who doesn't know you personally and doesn't know how aggravating the person you're dealing with is (imagine a lawyer assessing the merits of the case to decide whether to take it on, or a jury member hearing the case). The more calm, reasoned, and rational you appear at every step, the less likely you are to be sued later, or to lose the case if you are sued. You want every piece of the written record to reflect your evenhanded, deliberate, understated reaction. Less is more.

Don't overexplain. Less is more in another sense as well. Well-educated people with strong powers of reasoning (a category that includes almost everyone in a university) like to explain things. Resist this urge. When, after going through the appropriate process, you must make a hard decision, do not lay out your reasoning in detail. Simply present your decision and the rule/process that supports it. If you go into a recital of your reasons, you are inviting a debate over the small points. If your decision is final, present it and let it stand on its own. Trust me on this. If the dispute does go further and leads to a grievance or a lawsuit, you want an official record that shows scrupulous adherence to the process, full opportunity for facts to be presented and heard fairly, and the final decision and the facts on which it rests. You do not want to defend your thought process or line of reasoning. Ever. This is not an academic debate or an opportunity to win friends or influence people. Nothing you say at this point is likely to persuade anyone. It's enough to have to defend your actions—don't put yourself in a position of having to defend your thoughts, too.

Crucial Legal Concepts

There are two other legal concepts you also need to know about: notice and due process. If you understand the basics of these two fundamental tenets of our legal system and are careful to pay attention to them, you are more likely to avert a lawsuit or to win it if it cannot be avoided.

Notice

Notice is a legal concept that means that you may, in hindsight, be judged by whether you "knew or should have known" about a problem. So, take the afternoon when a faculty member wanders by your office to tell you about a conversation she had "the other day" with a female graduate student. According to the faculty member, this student reported feeling harassed by a visiting professor in the department. The student says the professor constantly asks her out, shows her unwanted sexual attention, and has hinted that she'll get an A in his class if she'll "spend some time" with him. The faculty member thinks you should take care of this.

You might be tempted to dismiss this information as gossip—after all, you didn't hear it directly from the student. But think again. The information you received, though second-hand, is an indication of possible sexual harassment. As a result, the university has arguably been "put on notice" of a possible problem and should take steps to address it. Don't, however, act without guidance. By all means, do not improvise what comes next: find out (or better yet, have found out in advance) who is the resource person for this kind of issue in your university's human resources or academic personnel office, and call that person—pronto—for advice. Sexual harassment is one of those areas in which the institution is liable for the actions of its employees and for actions taken after just about anyone in authority "knew or should have known" of the situation. Taking appropriate action now can greatly reduce (even eliminate) the university's potential liability. And yours. So, in a case like this you need to know that there is a possible legal issue, that it's your job to address it (no ostrich behavior, no matter how appealing it might be), and that you need guidance for what you do next.

Due Process

Due process is a concept that trips off the tongue of Americans, as it's central to our concept of government and democracy. To us, it's about "being fair." Not very many of us actually know what it means and requires in practice, though. Boiled down to its essence, due process means that, before you take action against someone, especially serious action that might affect the person's job or career (say, as in a student's dismissal), you inform that person about the problem and give him an opportunity to respond to whatever evidence you are using to make your decision. Most concepts of due process also include giving the person at least one opportunity to appeal a decision that goes against him to a decisionmaker who was not involved in the original proceedings.

In practice, this means that if a faculty member or student is charged with a serious violation of a university policy that might affect her status (working or studying at the university, for example), she should be told (given notice of) what the charges are and have an opportunity to respond to the evidence against her. The more serious the charge, the more formal should be the notice and the opportunity to respond. Thus, a charge of violating academic integrity that might lead to dismissal would probably require written notification of the charge and the evidence, with a full opportunity to respond in person, or in writing, or both. Most academic integrity proceedings involve a committee, and the accused person is notified of the committee's composition (and often permitted to object to any member on grounds of personal bias or conflict of interest) and given a chance to meet with the committee to discuss the evidence and to submit a written statement or information—and all this must be considered in full before a final decision is made. If the decision is that the findings are serious enough to warrant dismissal, the safest course, which your legal staff will undoubtedly advise you to take, is once again to provide notice: notify the person that dismissal is contemplated and offer her an opportunity to respond by submitting any mitigating information that the decisionmaker should consider before taking action. After the decision is made, an opportunity to appeal is often provided, though this is not mandatory.

Again, put yourself in the shoes of the person being accused. What would it take for you to feel that the proceedings were fair? You would want to be able to respond to all the evidence against you, to make your best case on your own behalf, and to feel that you were fully heard. To make your best case, you would need to know in advance what the possible consequences were, so that you would prepare your response with the proper level of seriousness.

Many of us think that the "right to confront witnesses" is a central tenet of due process. People envision a Perry Mason moment. (At least if they're old enough, they do. I don't know the names of the current generation of dramatic TV lawyers, but I hope you get the idea.) Actually, the central right is to confront the *evidence* and to have a chance to rebut it. Thus not every proceeding requires confrontation of witnesses, especially as one moves away from the kinds of criminal cases dramatized on TV to the internal administrative proceedings of universities. For example, in situations where the primary evidence is documentary (say, in a plagiarism case), there's no requirement that the accused person have the opportunity to confront the person who brought the matter to light: the requirement is that the person whose conduct is in question have the full opportunity to know about and to respond to all the evidence. This is widely misunderstood, even by lawyers who practice in other fields—say the criminal lawyer who is contesting the F his son got for turning in a paper bought on the internet, and who wants to be able to cross-examine in a full-blown hearing the teaching assistant who discovered the violation. It is, however, the rule that applies.

Naturally, due process plays out in many different ways, especially if you work in a public university, where any action taken is considered "state" or government action. We have more safeguards against government actions against us than we do in interactions among and between completely private parties. But even in a private university, basic due process concepts will be applied, to ensure that the decisions that are made are defensible and robust.

In summary, then, legal problems that come up in your professional life require some basic knowledge, but not of the law—only of when to call for help instead of acting on your own. Remember: anything having to do with personnel decisions (hiring, remediation, firing), compliance (especially with federal regulations or any laws), students' career issues (entrance, being terminated from a program), or the frictions between people (grievances, and so on) are grist for the legal mill. Find the policies, find the resource people, get advice, and follow it. Adhere to the process, and document every step   even if that simply means noting the date, the people involved, and the action. Keep it firmly in mind that these are arenas in which others may quickly be drawn in to scrutinize your actions and second-guess your decisions.

Let's look at a few situations that you might encounter. After reading each scenario, but before reading its discussion, ask yourself two questions: (1) What are the issues involved? (2) Who is your resource person for advice in this situation?

Personnel Issues

You have just been named as department head. You have had the same secretary for some years and would like to take her

along to your new position. However, there is already a secretary assigned to the department head's office. What do
you do?

In most colleges and universities, a department head has the authority to reassign employees within the unit—as long as each reassigned employee has the relevant qualifications, and as long as the
appropriate process is followed without any taint of discrimination.
That process will be more elaborate in some places, especially those
with a civil service system of some sort, than in others. In this instance, you may be able to keep your long-term secretary and reassign your predecessor's secretary to some other spot in the department.

However, you should first think through all the implications of
such an action. Will taking your secretary with you be in the
best interest of the unit? Will current working relationships suffer?
While your secretary may be excellent at supporting your research
efforts, will she be as skilled at supporting you in your new administrative responsibilities? What messages will others take from this
change—especially from your making the decision unilaterally before you've even officially started your new job? Are there others
working with either secretary who should be consulted or, at least,
informed before you make changes?

Before taking any action, consult with the office that deals with
support staff to find out what rules and procedures apply and to
hear any suggestions or advice that may be offered. There may not
be a legal issue here, but there is certainly a policy issue that, if not
handled correctly, could lead to a legal issue.

As the new dean, you evaluate your office's operations and
find that you really don't need four secretaries, but you do

need some accounting technicians and a business manager. You tell two of the secretaries that you are changing their responsibilities, and you assign them the accounting and business tasks. Now that they are no longer doing secretarial tasks, you call the personnel office and ask how to change their titles and give them pay increases. How do you think the personnel office will respond?

Before you act, you need to know what rules apply. Your institution may have both qualification requirements for those who take on new responsibilities and rules about open applications or access when new positions are created. You chose two of the four secretaries for the newly created jobs, but you gave none of them the choice of whether to apply for those jobs. You may have effectively split your staff into haves (higher pay, different duties) and have-nots (same old jobs, same old salary). If anyone is aggrieved, you may find yourself facing charges of discriminatory or arbitrary action.

Again, the office that deals with support staff is your resource and source of guidance. You may or may not have the power to make the changes or to provide higher salaries, depending upon the rules of the game within your institution. Check first, to avoid embarrassing backtracking and bad feelings.

A nonfaculty professional employee comes to you and expresses concern about her latest job evaluation. She explains that her new supervisor has made comments about her age and his perception that she is no longer "up to the task" of performing her duties. She always received good evaluations from her previous supervisors. How should you address her concern?

This employee is expressing an allegation of possible age discrimination. Inform her that you will look into the matter and get back to her. Also, you probably should provide her with a copy of the university's internal grievance procedures and advise her that she may file a grievance regarding her allegation. To avoid any appearance that you are retaliating against her for speaking against her supervisor, keep in mind that it is extremely important to avoid saying anything that she may interpret as meaning that you are not interested in her concerns or that you are not supportive of her filing a grievance. You should also notify the appropriate personnel office or the legal staff about your conversation with her.

Your resource in this situation is the personnel or human resources office that deals with employees in this woman's job category. Another resource might be the affirmative action or equal opportunity office. If your institution doesn't have such an office, call the office to which you report and/or the legal staff, depending on local culture: in some places, calling the legal staff directly would be expected; in others, it would be considered an end run around normal channels. Know your culture, but also know that there is a legal issue here in which you may get caught if you are not alert and careful.

> A faculty member comes to you and states that, because of his
> depression, he cannot teach any classes that begin before
> eleven a.m. He explains that it is difficult for him to wake up
> early, and that he and his psychologist feel that it is reasonable
> to teach later classes. Do you honor his request?

This is a legal issue, almost completely controlled by interpretations of the federal Americans with Disabilities Act (ADA), which covers a wide range of disabilities including mental health issues, and by the laws of your state. The way this faculty member phrases his request—providing a diagnosis, depression, and citing a clinician's advice—means that, under the ADA, he is asking for an accommodation for his disability. This is not a time for you to play armchair lawyer.

Your university probably has procedures in place to handle such requests, and the institution may be liable if they are handled improperly. As a result, you should avoid acting on this request until you have discussed the matter with the appropriate university office. This will be either the personnel office, its equal opportunity spin-off, or the legal office. If you take it upon yourself to grant a request without consulting the correct office, it is quite likely that you will inadvertently commit the institution to more of an accommodation than is required or appropriate, or to providing an accommodation when none is required. Once an accommodation has been provided, it becomes virtually impossible to reassess later and say that it was not appropriate; you may have committed the university to an incorrect position from which there is no retreat. Only at the last minute, once, did I hear of a department that was considering a request that a graduate student not have to take any courses requiring logical thinking, as his counselor had diagnosed him with a "logical processing deficit." The ADA does not mean you must grant every request. This one, for example, would have meant having to alter essential functions or requirements of the program, which the law does not require. The request does mean that a formal, prescribed process is triggered which must be documented at every step. But at no point should you act without competent and well-informed advice, because denying a legitimate request risks placing you and your institution in violation of the

ADA. The dean who denied a request for scheduling accommodations for a woman undergoing a course of chemotherapy learned this the hard way.

> When you assumed your new position as department chair, you inherited both your predecessor's corner office and his administrative secretary, a woman with a record of reprimands and a reputation for not getting along with anyone in the department. Your colleagues have made it clear that they are expecting you to get her out of the department. You call someone in the personnel office and inform him that the secretary has to be out of your office by tomorrow. What happens next?

Yes, I keep advising you to consult with the personnel office and other institutional resources. Your life as a faculty member probably did not incline you to see these folks as resources, if you even knew they existed. But exist they do, and in most places they have tremendous assistance to offer you. Make it a point to inform yourself about the resource they represent and how they can help you in your new role.

What will happen next? It depends. If you are in a public institution that has a civil service system, and/or an institution with a unionized support staff, firing someone may not be easy: civil service rules and union contracts provide certain rights to employees. The staff of the personnel office will work with you to find a resolution that serves the best interests of you, your department, and the employee. Addressing the problems may involve counseling the employee, going through the formal discipline process, or working with other campus units to place the employee in another job.

This situation should be a reminder that issues of employee performance should be addressed in their earliest stages, and generally with the assistance of the personnel office, before problems reach the crisis level. This case should also be a reminder that administrators should not intentionally leave personnel problems for their successors to address.

A professional employee is working irregular hours. Some nights she comes back in and works until midnight; the next day she may not arrive at the office until noon. She also spends time in the library doing research, and lately has been away from the office a good deal of the time. Both faculty and staff members have complained about her irregular schedule and her absences during normal work hours. What should you do?

The hours and work plans for any professional employee should have been agreed upon in advance, with the understanding that professionals are paid for the work performed, according to the needs of the unit, not by the hour. And the agreement should have been made known to others in the department. It appears that in this case others are not aware of how the employee's work is contributing to the department. If you approve of the employee's hours, you should communicate to all staff about the different ways in which different individuals contribute and let them know that her hours have your approval. You should also review her schedule and work plans periodically to ensure that they continue to meet the needs of the department. If you do not approve of her irregular hours, then you will need to start the process of stating your expectations and enforcing them, if necessary, through progressive disciplinary measures.

Flexible hours and work locations are becoming more common

with advances in technology and changes in employee expectations. Check with the personnel or human resources office to get advice about your scheduling plans and to find out whether your institution has policies on these matters.

> A group of university painters are working in your department. You begin to hear complaints from some female faculty, staff, and students that the painters continually talk to one another, loudly, about women. It doesn't appear that their comments are of a sexual nature, but nevertheless they are derogatory toward women. You know that sexual harassment is illegal, but this doesn't seem to fit into that category. What do you do?

Despite the lack of overtly sexual comments, the painters may be creating a hostile environment based on gender. Once you are put on notice of a potential problem in the area of civil rights, the university must take the appropriate action. The university's liability is often tied to how quickly and appropriately it acts when it "knows or should have known" of a problem.

Your resource here may be the personnel/human resources office, the equal opportunity office, or the legal staff. Don't delay. Consult with the relevant office right away. This *is* your problem whether it feels like it or not.

> Your department requires all professional employees to work at least one Saturday a month during the annual two-month fundraising drive. In compensation, they are allowed to take off either the Friday before or the Monday after their working Saturday. An employee informs you that because of his religious beliefs he cannot work on any Saturday. He complains

that his supervisor has told him that everyone must follow
the same rules and that he cannot be an exception. What do
you do?

This employee is requesting a religious accommodation. This is,
again, a legal matter. You should contact your personnel office or
legal staff for advice on how to proceed. Please keep in mind that,
as with a request for an accommodation for a disability, it's always
best to contact the appropriate university office before denying,
granting, or altering a request for an accommodation.

Student-Related Issues

A student comes to you to complain that her professor has no
syllabus and keeps changing the assignments and grading criteria. She is very frustrated and wants you to do something.

You need to know what written policies are in place in your department and/or college. The instructor may be leaving himself
open to charges of capricious grading if it is true that he has no syllabus and the requirements change. Before taking any action, you
need to interview him to see if the information provided by the
student is accurate. Once you have collected the relevant facts, seek
advice from the college office or the academic policy office.

A mother calls you and asks you what her son's grades are this
semester. She is worried that the young man is not taking his
studies seriously. Do you give her the information?

Under federal law (the Family Educational Rights and Privacy
Act, or FERPA), university staff cannot furnish such information to

parents unless the parents provide either documentation that they claimed the student on their federal income tax return for the immediately preceding year, or a signed consent form from the student authorizing the release of the information. It is best to explain this to the mother and refer her to the dean of students or another student-support office; you can be sure that that office has dealt with this issue many, many times and is prepared (better than you are) to handle the fallout from the mother's request, as well as to provide helpful advice to the concerned parents. It would also be wise to consult your institution's FERPA policy.

> You have recently been told by several students and trusted faculty members that a third-year assistant professor has been giving significantly higher grades to students who help her with tasks unrelated to her classes (babysitting, mowing her lawn, and so on). When you talk to the assistant professor, she indignantly denies these reports. You consult your advisory committee, which recommends not renewing the assistant professor's appointment. You must decide whether to follow the committee's recommendation. What factors should you consider?

You should discuss this situation with your dean. If the assistant professor has not had sufficient opportunity to respond to the allegations, any action you take will be vulnerable to later challenge. The dean's office or a higher academic policy unit, such as the provost's office, can advise you whether the process you have used is sufficient, and how to proceed from here. If the advisory committee has not used a fair and defensible process, that office will help you structure a process to collect and review the relevant facts and to develop the necessary documentation.

> Additional facts: Let's say you didn't consult the dean or the provost and simply authorized the nonrenewal of the assistant professor's appointment. You are a white man. The assistant professor is a woman and is also in a protected minority class. She has an excellent teaching and research record. Shortly after she receives official notification that she will not be reappointed, she approaches you and says: "I'm going to sue you and the university. You have violated my due process rights and discriminated against me because of my race and gender. I'll see you in court." Three months later, you are served with a summons and complaint naming you as a defendant in a federal lawsuit. What do you do?

Uh oh. You have a problem, and it's not trivial. Did you really think this situation would go away? Without stopping to do anything else, you must call your university's lawyers and then take the summons to them. Right away. Sooner, if possible. Any action involving termination of employment should be done in consultation with appropriate offices, starting very early in the process. At a minimum, this will involve the college office and the human resources department. Take the advice of your institution's lawyers very, very seriously. Make time to be responsive to their requests. Do not do anything without advice at every step from the lawyers. They are likely to ask you for your files—the originals, not copies. Although it may seem harmless to "tidy up" your files before providing them to counsel, this is unwise and possibly unethical or illegal. It is clearly in your, and your employer's, best interest for the lawyers advising you to have a complete and unvarnished view of the situation.

> An undergraduate comes to you and says that a graduate assistant has made what he believes to be very inappropriate remarks about his race. He tells you that, during class, the graduate assistant seems to treat white students better than he treats everyone else. In addition, he says that his and other African American students' grades have been consistently lower all semester. What do you do?

The undergraduate is making an allegation of racial discrimination. Advise him that the university takes such concerns very seriously. You will need to know about and be able to direct the student to the specific policies and procedures in place to address such concerns. For example, you may wish to tell him that the dean of students handles complaints of alleged discrimination between students. As with most situations, a quick and appropriate acknowledgment is better than leaving the person hanging without a response. You probably should also give the student a copy of the relevant pamphlet about filing complaints before he leaves your office.

> While reviewing graduate assistant appointments, you discover that one of the students has been here seven years, has yet to take his prelims, and appears to be making little progress toward his degree. Your institution has a five-year limit before prelims must be taken, and has annual progress-to-degree requirements. The student's advisor of record has recently taken a job at another university and will be leaving within the month. You are aware that the student has had

problems, from missed deadlines to aggressive and inappropriate challenges to faculty members at seminars, and that no
one else on the faculty will want to serve as his advisor. What
do you do?

Find out who in your institution you can call for advice and support. It's likely to be someone in the graduate college or the provost's office. Seek out your department's written policies on progress toward degrees, and descriptions of the program the student is
in. If these materials commit your department to providing an advisor, rather than making it incumbent upon the student to be accepted by an advisor, this situation will be more complicated to resolve. This is yet another reason to review your policies early in
your new job, and to learn enough about them to be comfortable
with them.

A first-year graduate student tells you she is having trouble
keeping up with her studies. She says that although she did
very well as an undergraduate, she is not able to hand in assignments on time and is unable to concentrate in class. She
has requested extra time to complete assignments, but her
professors are not willing to grant extensions. She tells you
that she has ADHD, but has never had any problems doing
her coursework because she takes medication. What is the
best course of action?

This student may or may not be asking for an accommodation
based on disability status. Again, this will be determined by interpretations of federal and state law—these scenarios play out daily
across the country. This is not a time to freelance or improvise. If
you do not already know the policies and procedures that apply to

these matters on your campus and the offices and individuals responsible for handling them, there's no time like the present for finding out.

Please keep in mind that when someone, like this graduate student, talks to you about a problem, you should not inquire about disability status—you are not a health professional (or, if you are, you are not in a privileged treating relationship with her); your concern is her conduct in your setting. However, if she volunteers that she has (or is worried that she may have) a disability, you are free to respond to that information. At that point, you must get guidance from your disability services office. Bear in mind, however, that the more you restrict your concern to your specific role—no matter how great your compassion or interest—the better off you will both be. Another person's private medical information is not your business. This is a specific boundary, and in your role you must not cross it. You can be compassionate, humane, and caring without opening this Pandora's box.

Since in this scenario the student herself brought up the topic of a disability, you may refer her to the office that supports students with disabilities. If she had not mentioned it, you would have sent her to the general student-support office, where there are staff members who will respond to her concerns—and who will have been trained to know when the legal threshold for a disability is reached. Then, if the student is granted an accommodation for a disability, do what is necessary to ensure that her professors provide the accommodation.

Professor McNabb's Sabbaticals

The instinctive response to an anonymous letter is often to throw it away. Unfortunately, you can't do that with the letter about Professor McNabb's lucrative sabbatical leaves. Because it makes specific allegations that are subject to verification, and that, if true, are serious violations of law or policy, you are now legally "on notice" and may be held to a higher standard of responsibility for all actions that occur after your "notice." This means that, however distasteful it may be, you need to show some degree of diligence in documenting your response to even an anonymous letter.

Anonymous letters are ugly. The common assumption is that honorable people don't write them or pay attention to them. Why not just throw it away? Well, the main issue to consider is whether a particular letter is simply scurrilous character assassination or whether it presents specific allegations. That is, does it just call someone a lying jerk, or does it say that last Tuesday he lied about his credentials to an audience of fifty people in room 240? Those are qualitatively very different letters to receive.

Even if it's simple character assassination, though, you might not want to throw it away. Think of the golden rule: if a colleague received anonymous letters about you, would you want to be told about them? What if the letter contained threats? However unpleasant or painful it might be, most of us would want to know if someone was angry enough to take such action against us. Thus, if the anonymous letter is just a mean-spirited attack, you still might want to show it to its victim, while offering your support and steering the person to resources in the institution that might be helpful—say the police or the employee assistance program. Think about the worst possible case, if the writer eventually escalated from letters to violence and the target got hurt. First, consider how you'd feel if you hadn't warned her that she should be on her guard and take steps to protect herself. Second, be aware that you might have incurred some liability by not passing along a warning. Few anonymous letters turn out to be precursors to violence, but this is not your risk to take or your choice to make.

As for the other type of anonymous letter, which provides specifics or references to events with many witnesses (like those fifty people in the audience in room 240 last Tuesday), the prudent response is to take steps (even if minimal) to investigate the allegations. It's quite likely that they're not true. But you won't know that—and won't be able to protect the innocent target—if you never check. Meanwhile, you should probably let the target know about the letter. Wouldn't you want to know that your department head had received such a letter about you and might have those thoughts in his or her head (regardless of whether the allegations were true or false)? Wouldn't you want an opportunity to respond or to explain or to put yourself on the record one way or the other?

In the case of the letter about McNabb's sabbaticals, you are in a double bind: annoying and thus risking the loss of Professor McNabb is no small cost, and there is nothing about this that she will receive gracefully. Nor will your dean be happy, as he has already signaled. In this situation, however, especially given the specificity of the information provided, you probably cannot avoid some level of fact-checking.

Some of the checking can be done very quietly, but at some point you are going to have to let McNabb know (1) that you got the letter and (2) that your duty is to do some basic verification/debunking. If either University A or University B is a public institution, it's probably a matter of public record whether McNabb was on salary there. Even so, it might be wise to have someone in your legal or personnel office (or even the provost or the dean) call his or her counterpart at the other university (especially if the two know each other) to pose the question. This is far more likely to have a hope of remaining quiet than if you call the department where McNabb worked: if you do that, McNabb is likely to hear within minutes that you're calling and checking, and the word may spread to others as well.

But steel yourself to the fact that either before or after you look into the facts, you're going to have to let McNabb know that you got the letter and did or are about to do some checking. You can assure her that you're doing it to protect her: people who feel compelled to write anonymous letters sometimes escalate their letter-writing campaigns until they see responses. If you can document definitively that neither institution paid Professor McNabb, then you'll be in a position to defend her—and she won't have to be distracted from her work—if the issue arises again in the future.

If the allegations turn out to be true, you may be able to offer McNabb an opportunity to correct the situation, although this is likely to be painful and to involve fairly large sums of money. You will absolutely have to involve those above you in the academic reporting chain, and the institution's lawyers, to sort this out. And at a public institution, just about anything you do is likely to be subject to public access through Freedom of Information or Public Record requests. Even at a private institution, word will probably seep out, especially if McNabb is disliked or has been abusive or disdainful of the accounting staff or others who may pull records or see letters about the situation.

Not all anonymous letters are motivated by nastiness or dislike. On the other side of the coin, a whistleblower might use an anonymous letter when he or she cares deeply about the institution but is too afraid of retaliation to speak out. This is another type of letter you shouldn't just toss in the wastebasket. Once someone feels desperate enough to send an anonymous letter, if it is ignored, the person may simply send the same or a similar letter to others: your Regents, the local media, and so on.

There's another way to think about this. If the allegations are true, and if you ignore them because they were brought to your attention in a form you find distasteful, you'll essentially be penalizing those who have complied with the rules all those years. If one person knows about this violation, it is highly likely that others will know, too. Secrets are hard to keep within organizations, and the fact that violations have been occurring and have been overlooked for reasons of status (or whatever) will corrode the goodwill and trust of the rule-followers in your department.

And there's something larger at stake here as well: the sabbatical tradition is not well understood outside academia (especially in hard economic times), and the risk here is that the sabbatical privilege across your university could be compromised by demonstrated maladministration or abuse of the privilege. There is nothing like an ugly scandal to bring down a system that's not well understood to begin with. If Professor McNabb has been abusing the system, and you avert your gaze, you will put at risk all the enhancement of teaching and research and service that could result from future sabbaticals—which might no longer exist at your institution. That's a pretty big price to pay, and you'll surely be long remembered for it.

It just may not be the legacy you hoped to leave.

Chapter 7

Violations

Emily Waters is a Ph.D. candidate. Her research is virtually complete and she anticipates defending her thesis next semester. She has come to you for confidential advice because you presided at the required graduate student ethics seminar last week.

Tense, disheveled, and bleary-eyed, Waters tells you that her advisor, Dr. Brian Pane, is always away attending meetings. She believes many of these are sponsored by drug companies, and suggests that he's probably getting "filthy rich" from the honoraria. Even when he is in town, she reports, Dr. Pane does not supervise his students, attends lab meetings irregularly, and during his cameo appearances seems preoccupied. The fact that he clips his nails during meetings proves this, she says. She wants to know if his behavior meets the department's standards for faculty.

You have been a little concerned about Pane's many absences and the number of his classes that are covered by guest lecturers. So this is not exactly news to you, but it is unwelcome, as you have so far managed to avoid having to deal with the issue.

While you are trying to figure out what to say, Waters becomes agitated and starts reciting a laundry list of complaints about Pane's conduct. Her accusations seem to you to have a frantic quality, a sort of manic fervor. She reminds you of a child trying to get attention.

One of her allegations is particularly serious. She tells you that she has tried unsuccessfully to duplicate results from an experiment that Dr. Pane reported and published, and that she has found two lab books: one with the same results as hers and another with numerous erasure marks and significantly different results. Both differ from Pane's published data. She says she is reluctant to give you copies of the lab book data, her results, and Pane's article, for fear that Dr. Pane will know she was the source. He chairs her thesis committee. She is unwilling to be the source of complaints against him, though she also says she is increasingly uncomfortable letting these concerns go.

The general take on Dr. Pane is that he is undoubtedly brilliant but volatile—he has an explosive temper and a cantankerous personality and is intolerant of questions. His social skills leave something to be desired. Yet he is highly influential in his field and over the years graduate students have lauded him as a mentor. Many of his former students are at the top of their field now. Furthermore, you have heard him complain about Ms. Waters: that her work is not of high quality and that she is unstable.

You do some discreet checking, trying not to reveal that your information comes from Waters. When you describe the situation to a close colleague, without naming names, she responds: "Is that Emily Waters again? She's crazy! We have a file a foot thick on her and her complaints against all her professors."

The line between the difficulties that inevitably arise when people work together and conduct that violates boundaries and is potentially damaging to the integrity of the group is an important one to be able to recognize. (In other words, you need to learn to separate the crooks from the jerks.) You will concentrate your time and energy largely on problems in the first category, from having to tell someone his or her work isn't meeting standards to dealing with bad chemistry between co-workers or clashing expectations about "how people act at work" to coping with downright boorish behavior from people who otherwise are strong contributors. But some problems go to the very heart of the integrity of the work and the place. Most of these fall into the category of academic misconduct, which includes such misdeeds as falsifying data, denying someone proper credit for published work, and using institutionally conferred power or position for personal gain.

Dealing with a full-blown, formal academic integrity inquiry or investigation is well beyond the scope of this book. Together with others, I developed a comprehensive how-to manual for such cases that includes checklists, sample letters, investigation casebooks, and the like. It was published by the American Association for the Advancement of Science under the title *Responding to Allegations of Research Misconduct*. Given the relative rarity of formal proceedings in this area, with any luck you will not need that sort of specialized knowledge during your term of service. If a case does present itself, you'll need all the skills in this book plus a few extra. My best advice is to consult with someone who has been through a case like this before—preferably more than one. There are a set of key points in an academic integrity proceeding at which the intuitive response is the wrong response: following your instincts will get you into trouble. Unless you have access to an experienced person who can steer you around the quicksand, even peripheral involvement in one of these sad situations can be unimaginably costly. With a strong grounding in principles and some expert guidance, you can survive a problem of research misconduct—or just allegations of same—in your environment. Fortunately, most of the questions and concerns that come up in universities do not rise to a level that requires formal proceedings: statistics are hard to come by, but by any measure, these cases are rare. Far more frequent are the types of disputes that are discussed in this chapter.

Recalibrating Your Compass

Let's face it: there is something about issues of research misconduct that causes administrators to lose their compass. In my experience, more of these cases "go weird" than any other type. My own theory is that, though we don't like to talk about it, most scholarly work is as much an art as a science. We don't want to acknowledge that research is messier than we like to think. Who hasn't wrestled with how to interpret data? Do I put this in, or leave it out? How can I make sense of what my student wrote? Even if I believe in the results, the notes are illegible, incomplete, and impossible to follow. . .

As a community we tend to lose our ability to think clearly when it comes to academic misconduct. In part, I think this is because, beyond the really clear cases (such as stealing someone's entire thesis), the rules tend to be pretty vague. I once sat in a misconduct proceeding with three National Academy–caliber scientists who said, at the end of the presentation of evidence, "Well, sure, it's sleazy and disgusting, but it's not misconduct."

Perhaps because of the "art" aspect of scholarship and because of the many gray areas in the norms, we tend to identify with those accused of misconduct. The "there but for the grace of God go I" factor kicks in—to the detriment of a strong process and sustainable outcomes. Every investigative committee I've ever worked with has seen members arrive at the second meeting a little bleary-eyed, saying: "I was up all night going over everything on my CV, wondering if any of my work could be accused of similar things." The propensity to identify with the parties in these cases can be disorienting and act like a magnet that distorts a compass.

And, of course, these problems usually stir up strong feelings, which, for people who've self-selected for careers of analysis and reflection, can be aversive in and of themselves.

So, for a lot of reasons, these cases are more difficult than many others. But remember: it's not about you. It is about the good of the whole, the department and the larger institution. This chapter is meant to help you recalibrate your compass.

In your leadership position you will have to acquire the knack for recognizing the signals of problems that may become extremely serious—the low-incidence, high-severity problems discussed in Chapter 5. Because these situations do not arise very often, it's easy to miss the early warning signs of something that could come to consume unpleasantly large chunks of your life.

Signals to watch for include any allegation that, if substantiated, would be extremely serious, no matter how implausible or unlikely sounding when first presented. They also include situations in which the playing field isn't likely to be level: where there is a large power imbalance between the parties. For instance, where one of the parties involved is so hot-tempered that others might withdraw solely because of high transaction costs, or where the personal relationships are clouded with current or past sexual intimacy, or, as in our example of Emily Waters and Dr. Brian Pane, where one party sits on the thesis committee of another. This category encompasses the kinds of allegations we talked about in Chapter 6 that would count as putting you on legal notice, like even a suggestion—no matter how ludicrous it seems to you—that a star faculty member is crossing personal boundaries or fudging data. In public institutions, it may also include uses of public funds for which special rules exist: when you can buy alcohol or expensive meals or gifts for people, for example. Think about what newspapers, federal regulators, auditors, and general busybodies might find to be of interest. (This is not to imply that all allegations will turn out to be true. But recognizing what category a given allegation falls in is key to knowing what steps to take next.) And remember, if you follow the guidelines outlined in this book, and keep your own squeamish feelings under control, you will be able to handle these problems—even if it's uncomfortable.

Many questions come up about authorship: who should get credit for contributions to scholarly publications. Questions about the handling of data also arise frequently. Other aspects of professional conduct spark questions as well: What about using institutional property? What about use (and abuse) of information received while reviewing manuscripts or proposals? What about mentoring and supervision of students? Graduate students perceive an enormous amount of exploitation or abuse of themselves and their colleagues. Sometimes this perception is accurate, and sometimes it isn't, but the students simply don't know the context or have access to sufficient information to develop a wise, complete, or reasoned assessment of the situation. What is your professional obligation when you discover or suspect possible misconduct in research? Are you obligated to report the possible problem? To confront the person about whose work you have concerns? All such questions, and particularly the ones that involve the education of students, are (or ought to be) vital to universities.

Without some clear thought, it's very easy to go astray in these areas. And acquiring that kind of clarity takes some application and study. Let's look at some of the types of situations that tend to recur.

Authorship and Attribution of Credit

In universities, the coin of the realm is recognition for scholarly contributions as recorded in publications. The vast majority (in my experience, up to 70 percent) of questions that come up about scholarly conduct involve the attribution of credit. Transgressions such as honorary authorship (assigning authorship to one who has not made any significant intellectual contribution to the work) and redundant publication (publishing the same work repeatedly without reference to previous appearances) do not necessarily rise to the level of plagiarism, but can be very serious nonetheless.

Basic tensions over credit can be exacerbated by disparities in practices across fields. It is important to be aware of these differences. For example, an English professor once told me that she had struggled with how to think about the respective contributions of coauthors when she served on campus committees, as she had never written anything with a coauthor in her entire career. The meaning of authorship and the ethical obligations that apply are very straightforward in her work. In high-energy physics, in contrast, scores if not hundreds of coauthors are not uncommon, and the ethical issues are not always so clear.

Also, norms of authorship are evolving, and someone whose early career was spent in a laboratory in which the principal investigator's name was on every paper that came out of his lab regardless of whether he had been involved in the work is quite likely to feel entitled to benefit from the practice when he or she achieves senior status. These are often strong feelings, not completely rooted in logic or rationality, and must be acknowledged, if not always honored. When someone comes to you with questions or complaints about attribution, taking the time to talk through the reasons for "good practice" is usually a worthwhile investment.

The most succinct statement of the emerging criteria for authorship (in every field but high-energy physics, which, the philosopher Bernard Gert once quipped, uses the criterion "If your name begins with a letter of the alphabet, you're an author") is that every person listed should have made a meaningful intellectual contribution to the work. As a rule of thumb for sorting out who falls into this category, the following test is often useful. To be an author, a person must (1) be able to defend the paper by explaining the work and responding to substantive questions about it; and (2) have participated in at least one of the following: conception of the work, collection of data, analysis of data, development of the manuscript.

Many problems will resolve themselves when the criteria are presented in this way. Ideally, the assumptions and expectations about what is required to qualify as an author will be discussed and understood before the initiation of the project. But that doesn't always happen, and even when it does happen, changes in circumstances over the life of the project may make the original agreements inappropriate or inapplicable when the time comes to attribute authorship.

Michael Green, a graduate student, shows you an editor's letter inviting his advisor, Professor Stotler, to contribute a chapter to an upcoming book. Scrawled across the bottom is a note in the professor's handwriting saying "Mike, take a stab at this.—RPS." Green also shows you several drafts of the chapter, which he says are his work. He points out the date on each draft, and marginal comments by Stotler making suggestions for revisions and additions. You can trace the evolution of the work, as each of these suggestions is incorporated in a successive draft. At the end of the most recent draft is a handwritten note: "Mike—this is fine. No more work will be necessary.—RPS."

Green says that his girlfriend, who works in the department office, typed a letter from Stotler submitting the chapter to the editor in his own name only. Green tells you that when he asked about this and requested credit as a coauthor, Stotler responded: "Oh, don't worry about that. This was a learning exercise. You'll get to coauthor things later." Green doesn't want any trouble with his advisor, but feels he has been unfairly deprived of credit for work he has done.

In your judgment this is not an "allegation" under the campus policy and federal misconduct regulations, but just an expression of concern. Therefore, you do not immediately invoke the inquiry procedure provided in the campus policy, but decide to gather more facts to determine whether an inquiry is warranted.

You call the previous department head, Jenny Hamm, for

advice. She reminds you that Stotler is a disorganized person who lets things fall through the cracks, but that he publishes prolifically and to wide acclaim. Stotler recently received two major honors in his field, and last year the department gave him a significant raise to counter an outside offer. Hamm says she can well believe that the inclusion of Green's name might have slipped through the cracks because Stotler is so over-committed, but that she's sure Stotler will make it right as soon as it is called to his attention.

Hamm also tells you that Green is known as a "champion whiner" and is currently on academic probation, an unusual status for a graduate student. She reports that Green came to her several times with complaints against faculty members, but didn't pursue them when she suggested appropriate channels for recourse.

Hamm recommends that you handle the matter quietly so as not to cause Stotler any embarrassment. She discourages initiation of an inquiry because she doesn't think anyone in the department could be neutral about Stotler: people either are his strong supporters or hate him.

You decide to do what you can to discourage Michael Green, but you give him a copy of the university policy and tell him about other resources on campus, including the research integrity officer and graduate college grievance dean.

This time, after much consultation with you, in which you make good use of Chapter 4's "key sentences" such as "What action do you seek from me?" Green does decide to pursue the matter. He files a complaint under the university's research integrity policy. A formal integrity inquiry ensues. The committee requests the submitted draft from the editor and compares it with the student's drafts. Though the titles are identical, there is no resemblance in content, structure, or prose style.

Professor Stotler, outraged at having been accused of one of academe's major crimes, tells the committee that Green's work was so bad that he threw it all out and wrote something hastily himself. He also indicates that he never discussed the flaws in the work with Green. His draft is judged by the inquiry team to be a completely independent intellectual effort.

In interviewing Stotler the committee discovers that other aspects of his interactions with students are far from ideal. At one point he exclaims about Green: "How was I to know he minded washing my car? I'd say, 'Mike, do you mind washing my car?' and he'd say 'No.'"

There were problems in this situation, but they did not amount to academic misconduct (although there was no way to be sure of that without investigating). There were problems of communication, problems of exploitation of a student, problems in the way the scholarly work in that group was done. But there wasn't a problem of misconduct under the federal regulations on fabrication, falsification, and plagiarism. (To put it another way, Professor Stotler was a jerk but not a crook.)

Note that Stotler's protestation that Mike had never objected to washing his car was the first anyone on the investigative committee had ever heard of it. Green had not mentioned anything about performing personal services for his advisor. This phenomenon—the discovery of egregiously inappropriate conduct that has not been reported by the complainant—is fairly common in formal investigations, and it reinforces the importance of basing decisions only on documented facts, not on personalities or status.

It is not surprising that the professor was furious at being accused of an offense that he would not have considered committing. Nevertheless, he had set himself up for the accusation by the way he conducted himself, and it didn't help that nobody had ever told him that. Nobody had ever said, "The manner in which you interact with your students is not acceptable in this university."

Even though, in this situation, there was no plagiarism or violation of standards of authorship, there were severe violations of the university's standards for graduate mentoring. In the real-life case on which I based this example, Professor Stotler's graduate faculty privileges were suspended by the dean of the college, because the department head was afraid to rock the boat with his prominent faculty member. (The department head stepped down at the end of the academic year, at the request of the dean.) The dean then required Stotler to meet with her monthly until she was satisfied that he met the institution's standards for membership in the graduate faculty. (This took almost two years.)

Michael Green was moved to another advisor to avoid Stotler's wrath. The new adviser had higher professional standing than Stotler, which provided a level of protection for Green in the job market against any possible whisper campaign or other retaliatory action that Stotler might attempt. And Green eventually got his degree. He found an academic job and now has tenure. I hope he is treating his own students well.

Had anybody in that department been talking about issues concerning graduate mentoring and good communication, and had there been better monitoring of Stotler's interactions with his students, there would not have been a misconduct review, which in this case would have been better for everyone. It is likely, given that most departments are small communities, that colleagues and the department head knew, on some level, that Stotler was not treating students appropriately, but no one was willing to confront him—including the person whose job it was to be the steward of the environment.

What follows are some variations on this theme of what is and what isn't academic misconduct regarding attribution of authorship.

> "My professor says he's taking this project away from me and giving it to someone else."

The student is sitting across the desk, often with a satchel full of laboratory notebooks, informal correspondence (email, handwritten notes, etc.) and other documents he sees as central to his case. The events he describes will vary, but the theme will be that he has worked on this project exclusively for a substantial period of time and that the professor has now informed him that someone else will be taking over. The student will almost invariably claim to know the reason for the change, even if his knowledge involves mind-reading. The reason he cites may come from a wide spectrum: his professor thought he wasn't making enough progress; he failed his prelims; they've had a falling-out; the project looks promising and the professor wants all the credit for himself; the professor never understood the idea before, but now that he does, he wants a more favored student to pursue it; and so on. The student has come to you because he wants to be given author credit on papers based on the project and to be protected from retaliation for raising the issue.

The best approach to this situation is to get the student's answers to a series of questions, pose the same questions to the professor, and then do a reality check. Most such situations can be resolved if there is general agreement on the answers. Even where there is not general agreement, the answers to these questions will usually point the way to a solution:

- Where did the idea for the project originate?
- What was said when the project began about authorship and/or outlets for the work?
- How long has the project been under way?
- Is it the student's thesis project?
- Is the project an isolated, narrow one, or integral to a larger (and/or long-term) project under way in the research group?
- How much of the work is complete?
- Who did the actual work? That is, who collected and/or analyzed the data? Who wrote the manuscript?
- How has the project proceeded: what are its major steps and their timing?
- How significant is the work to the field?

In personality clashes and misunderstandings, it is often good practice to encourage the parties to speak directly to each other. Often, and particularly if they are of unequal status (such as student and professor), it can be helpful to have a third party involved in the conversation. Try to make the meeting as nonthreatening as possible for all participants. Ways to do this can include holding the meeting in a neutral setting, discussing contentious issues in a manner that is not accusatory and does not imply that conclusions have already been reached, and focusing on the common ground of the participants.

Speaking of informal resolution efforts, it is important that you be sure the limits of these efforts are understood at the outset. In addition, you must provide a clear and careful explanation of the policies and procedures that will apply if the informal efforts do not succeed. It should include when those policies and procedures will begin to apply, who will decide whether and when to initiate a formal procedure, what the role of each of the parties will be, and who will know what each has said.

If the parties have had an irreconcilable rupture in their personal relationship, it is often necessary to develop a written agreement recording the resolution of the matter. Such an agreement should be signed by the disputants and the go-between and filed officially in the department's files, including the personnel or student file of each of the disputants. Its contents might include:

- a brief recapitulation of the history of the matter;
- a statement of the interests of each of the parties;
- a statement about who will be an author of what, under what conditions, in what period of time;
- guidelines as to how future work will be apportioned (will each party continue working with the data? in the general area? and so on);
- if manuscripts are to be developed, how the drafts will be reviewed by each party, and within what time limits;
- what will happen if any party fails to live up to his or her obligations.

> "The postdoc who did all this work is gone and there's no way to reach her. We need to write up the work because my grant is up for renewal. How do we do this properly?"

This comes up surprisingly often. The person raising the question senses that it might not be right to make the absent person the first author, because she won't have an opportunity to see and revise the manuscript, but it feels equally wrong to omit her name entirely. Both instincts are correct: it is not proper to list someone as an author (particularly as first author) unless that person has endorsed the manuscript. Similarly, it is not proper to present work without giving credit to a person who did much of it.

The first step is to make another effort to track down the absent person. In some circumstances, this is simply not possible: she may have died, had a nervous breakdown, or gone trekking in the Himalayas to recover from the stress of working in that laboratory. More often, however, she is simply not answering her former colleague's calls or letters because their personal relationship has eroded. (This is a polite way of describing the most typical case, in which they've had a big fight and neither ever wants to see the other again.) If she is found, use the approach described above, and develop a written agreement governing the development of the manuscript.

The second step, if she is completely unreachable, is to communicate with the editors of the journal to which the manuscript is to be submitted and the program officer at the funding agency. Describe the situation and work out a mutually acceptable solution. Usually this involves a special acknowledgment or note describing the circumstances, presented in an agreed-upon format. Rarely (usually when the primary author has died), it may be appropriate to list the absent person as the first author, but with a note explaining the reason, such as that the manuscript was developed after her death.

> "I've been using the same method for years. To avoid a charge
> of plagiarism or duplicate publication, do I have to write a
> new methods section every time I publish? This seems like a
> waste of effort."

This question invariably arises after someone has read about or encountered a case of plagiarism, when he gets to pondering his own work. The answers to questions like this hinge on the compact between author(s) and the reader: What will the reader assume (in this journal, in this field) about an article? Any time the situation deviates from what the reader is likely to assume, the reader should be signaled.

In most scholarly publications, this compact entitles the reader to assume that work presented under a name or set of names is original work performed by the listed individuals, and that it makes some new contribution to the state of knowledge in that field. There are exceptions, such as literature reviews and personal essays, but by and large this is the norm.

Depending upon the field, the reader may or may not expect a methods section to be written anew with each publication. To be absolutely clear and aboveboard, an author should inform the journal editor that the methods section is the same or similar to one published previously, but the results and discussion are entirely novel. In many fields, the editor is unlikely to find this a problem (if the author is terribly resistant to raising the question with the editor, it's a good sign that this situation needs more thought and scrutiny). Alternatively, a footnote to the methods section can cite prior appearances. Note that permission from the first publisher or copyright holder may be required if the methods section is a large enough portion of the work.

Data-Related Problems

There are also many questions about the application and interpretation of data that come up repeatedly: What are appropriate practices for recording and retaining data? If data are generated or collected automatically by high-tech equipment, what standards apply for recording and retention? Must every datum ever generated be retained? In what form? What if the data are a decade old and the equipment that generated them is obsolete? When is it okay to disregard outliers? What are the standards for their exclusion?

Concerns about such issues don't necessarily amount to allegations of misconduct. I have been approached by many students who say something along these lines: "We did this experiment and my adviser looked at it and said we wouldn't use those runs, but only used others. He's throwing away data; it must be fraud." When I point out that there are many reasons to discard data, and ask whether the student has discussed these matters with the adviser, I am frequently told, "Oh, no. In my lab you don't ask." The problems here may be not misconduct but merely poor communication or ambiguity about applicable standards. (Then again, a situation that begins with such questions may also reveal a more serious problem.)

In my experience, questions about proper standards for recording and retaining data are rare. However, questions about access to and control of data or results are the second-most-common category of appeals, after those about authorship and attribution of credit. In many ways these two categories are variations on the same theme, since the underlying issue usually centers around who will benefit from the work. Many of these problems can be avoided or solved with the following guidelines:

- The university should have a rule about ownership of and access to data.
- Students should always be able to take copies of their own lab notebooks. (Many professors are resistant to this idea, but they have to learn to live with it. Fair is fair.)

- Sometimes it's necessary to develop a formal agreement about who will be able to pursue various lines of research.

"The postdoc took primary data when he left the university."

This comes up with regularity; when I was a campus research standards officer (the front line for dealing with allegations of research misconduct), I encountered this kind of situation about four to six times a year. Depending upon the personal relationships between the individuals involved, the first step is usually to ask for the return of the data. It's surprising how many researchers don't think of this on their own.

If this obvious step has not been taken, it's worth asking why. Did it simply not occur to the researchers, or are there other difficulties in the situation? The most frequent underlying issue is that there is some friction between the principal investigator and the person who took the data over the way the data will be written up or interpreted. In that case, you may need to do more groundwork before you take any action.

Departing individuals take data for a variety of reasons; if a person's reason can be determined, the response should be calibrated to that reason. It may be that he just didn't know any better. The response to this is straightforward: a polite phone call or letter explaining that the data are owned by the university and requesting the return of the primary data. Offer to make copies of notebooks and so on for him, or urge him to make his own copies before returning them. Alternatively, if it appears from your initial queries that he did it to protect himself or for personal advantage, you may need advice from your legal staff. Even here, the first step is likely to be a request for the data's return, but it may need more formal trappings and you will need guidance on subsequent steps if your first request is rebuffed.

Deciding whether a particular expression of concern does or does not amount to an allegation of misconduct is a challenge. Many questions that are raised about academic practice turn out, once examined, to be results of misunderstandings, miscommunications, or personality clashes. Most can be settled through direct conversation or mediation. Some concerns are serious but do not relate to research integrity. The ones that require investigation or fall within a university policy (say, sexual harassment or discrimination) should be referred to the appropriate office for handling.

However, if the allegations are about the integrity of research and the matter is handled entirely informally, this can leave the person accused of misconduct in a very awkward situation later. The accused person can be cleared unequivocally only if she has no opportunity to alter the data after the concerns are first expressed. Depending upon the nature of the allegation, you may need to consider mechanisms for securing copies of the data very early in the process. This can be enormously upsetting to the person accused, so it is a good idea to explain carefully why you are securing copies of the data—in order to leave him better protected at the end of the process.

In general, if an expression of concern is received by a faculty member, the faculty member needs to know that he should at least inform the department head unless the concern is obviously frivolous, mistaken, or the product of miscommunication. This advice applies to expressions of concern that clearly touch upon extremely serious matters addressed by institutional or legal regulations, including scientific misconduct, plagiarism, fabrication or falsification of data, compliance requirements, and crimes. Concerns that fall into those categories should be, from the beginning, handled with extreme care, and you as department head should ensure that the institutional officials responsible for compliance or the implementation of applicable policy are consulted. Those officials may or may not be involved in the eventual solution, but you need to consult them, because if the matter proceeds to a full-blown case, it will be important to have responded appropriately from the outset. This is a stage where a great deal can go wrong for all parties if things are not managed carefully.

These determinations are judgment calls. The factors to be considered include the potential seriousness of the allegations, the history of questions about the conduct of the individual concerned, and an assessment of the personalities of the parties. Caution is essential. Even professionals with outstanding reputations have been guilty of misconduct, and accusers with unstable personalities have been correct. (The shorthand expression for this is "Even flakes can be right.")

The more serious the allegations, or the potential allegations, the more formally things should be handled. It is important to keep in mind that a formal and documented proceeding can offer better protection to an innocent faculty member who may be a victim of a vendetta or other malice. Finally, if any of the parties is particularly volatile or appears unstable, the situation warrants especially careful handling.

Adding Sex to the Mix

Let's move on to a category of problems that can be even tougher to handle: problems of academic conduct complicated by sex. By now, having read the earlier chapters of this book, you should be acutely aware, at least in principle, of the importance of boundaries, including sexual boundaries, and of the possible legal consequences of not paying attention to such issues. All this should be helping you to think more clearly about what is and is not your business with respect to intimate relationships. Still, when you are the leader charged with the good of the department as a whole, you are responsible for providing guidance in this area, however uncomfortable that responsibility might be. This responsibility can be lessened if your institution has an effective all-campus training program that sets boundaries and provides information about situations that may arise and how to respond to them professionally and appropriately. But it is your duty, in one way or another, to sensitize those who have positions of power over others (read: just about everyone except the undergraduates) to their perceived power and its potentially pernicious effects.

Stop here for just a moment and recognize that the closeness that develops between people who work hard together can be both stimulating and, at times, highly erotic. Of course, some people are more susceptible to such feelings than others, but it's a good starting place to acknowledge that it can be fun and engaging and intense to work closely with someone.

Sometimes, though, this intensity spins out of control. This is when it pays to know your institution's policy about consensual sexual relationships between faculty and students or between teaching assistants and their students. Most of us understand that it's possible to become good friends with a person and still assess that person professionally, properly, and objectively. So long as there isn't a sexual relationship, your ability to be objective is a call you are left to make for yourself. However, there is a conflict of interest involved in assessing the work of someone with whom you have an intimate personal connection. (That's a euphemism for sex, by the way.) Once sex enters the picture, a societal boundary has been crossed and objectivity is considered out of the question.

Two colleagues come to see you. They are concerned about the behavior at on- and off-campus seminars by a distinguished professor visiting from a European research institute. They report that Professor Geoff has been challenging the results presented by an advanced Ph.D. student in the department, Grace Lee. Lee, a woman from Asia, is somewhat shy, and many members of the department have been helping her prepare for these public presentations, which are difficult for her. While your colleagues believe there is some merit to Geoff's challenges of her methodology and results, his criticisms are so aggressive and so personal that the events are very uncomfortable for the audiences—let alone for Lee. At a recent meeting in another state, Lee was seen talking with the police after her presentation. Your colleagues ask you to get Professor Geoff to tone down his behavior.

When you meet with Geoff, he becomes agitated and pours out grievances against Lee and her husband, saying he wants to file charges of theft of his intellectual property and violations of academic integrity in publication. He reports that he and Grace Lee had a short consensual fling that is now over. He has no supervisory authority over her; they met when she sought him out for advice about the application of his techniques to her work. He says that when they were lovers he provided her with unpublished data and other cutting-edge information, and that she and her husband have just published much of that data in an article in which he is not mentioned.

You then meet with Lee and learn that she has just filed

sexual harassment charges against Professor Geoff at the Equal Opportunity Office. She admits that they had a consensual affair, but she reports that when she tried to end it he wouldn't accept her decision. She says he is now stalking her. She wants you to protect her.

Now what? In this situation, there's no formal supervisory relationship, which helps in one dimension, but the likelihood of cultural complications and different mores is high. So, going back to your obligation to set the tone and to sensitize members of your department about such issues, when Professor Geoff arrived to take up his visiting position, was he given any information or guidance about the grievance climate in American universities and the potential risks involved in relationships with students? (We'll leave aside the student's marriage here, as, truly, you are not being asked to become the bedroom police.)

The warning sign here is the interlocking intimate relationships. Take my advice and follow formal procedure from the beginning: there is nothing about this situation that you are likely to be able to resolve happily through informal efforts. Let those who are paid for dealing with allegations of discrimination and/or misconduct guide every step you take.

But what about the next scenario? It's one in which your instincts might lead you astray because of the special culture of an academic environment.

Five undergraduate women come to meet with you, complaining that Professor Keane makes jokes and remarks of a sexual nature in a 100-level class. For example, he illustrated a lecture with slides of nude women. The students quote comments Keane has made about female students' clothes and appearance: "That's a nice sweater." "You look tired. Were you up all night making love?" They say he does not make similar comments to male students. He also talks about his divorce and recent dating experiences. The students report that he makes such remarks several times in every class period.

Professor Keane has tenure. The class has 100 students. There are six weeks to go in the semester. As far as you can tell, the sexual jokes, comments, and examples have nothing to do with course content. The students demand that Keane be replaced immediately.

Again, this has all the hallmarks of a situation in which you do not want to act on your own, because of the complexity of the issues and because of the large power differential between the tenured faculty member and the undergraduates. Process is your friend. Call the appropriate campus office for assistance. It may be necessary to channel this through the discrimination and harassment procedure, but because it involves classroom speech, each and every step will require both legal and policy oversight. The students are presenting this as a complaint about "sexual comments," but because it involves the content of remarks made in a classroom setting, Keane's academic freedom will almost certainly be invoked. As you know by now, it is not the case that every remark made in a classroom is protected by academic freedom, but the time and place will make this situation vastly more complicated to handle than if it had happened, say, in the hallways or the cafeteria.

Some problematic situations involving sexual relationships, for example, those involving low-key or minor allegations, and those involving individuals who are otherwise on cordial terms, and those where allegations have not arisen previously, may be reasonable candidates for informal intervention or mediation efforts for a short period of time. However, if they are not resolved quickly, within a week or two at most, it is probably appropriate to invoke institutional policy and follow its strictures.

An Ounce of Prevention

I hope that, having read these examples and case studies, you are now better able to recognize which issues fall into the category of academic misconduct rather than, say, the category of purely personnel matters. Recognizing which category a problem falls into is key to knowing what steps to take next.

I also hope that reading all these examples hasn't made you feel overwhelmed or discouraged. Don't let these cases get you down. You can handle them. Just follow the advice you've read in this book and don't let the problems unsettle you. Take a deep breath, and remember that your job is to keep the greater good of your department and your institution in mind. Now read the following guidelines, which will help you stay on course.

First of all, preferably at a time when you do not have a current problem brewing, think about tone setting. The more you can sensitize everyone to standards of good conduct, the better off all will be. When a problem does arise, always take reasonable precautions as soon as warning signs surface. If you hear about something falling into one of the categories outlined earlier in this chapter, make a note of it, the date on which you heard it, who said it, and what you did in response. (Your response should always include consulting with someone who has knowledge and authority of which policy will be involved if an allegation or complaint is filed or if later it is proven that a violation has been committed.) Put your note either in a file you open for this particular situation or in one where you keep records of various administrative items. Make sure you'll be able to find it if you need it. Here's an example of this kind of note:

> Professor Johnson asked me at the department coffee on Thursday, March 21, 2006, to "handle" a situation that her grad student Maria Porter faces: how to turn down persistent requests for dates from visiting professor George Knowlton. Called the ombudsman's office for advice. Was referred to dean of students, who will have a staff member seek out Maria and interview her. [Date/your initials]

The adage about an ounce of prevention being worth a pound of cure applies in this area with a vengeance: unresolved problems in these categories have a tendency to turn messy. Some such problems may go away if ignored, but more often they will fester in unhealthy ways. I know of an institution in which the compilation of a set of metrics for self-study revealed that a certain department's attrition rate for female graduate students was almost twice that for male students and was significantly higher than those in peer departments at other institutions. Investigation showed that two of the department's influential faculty members were widely perceived to treat women students unfairly. Further, it emerged that their grad students counseled one another not to do anything other than try to transfer when the treatment became unbearable, because the department head had a policy of refusing to meet with any student who had not first talked to the faculty member involved. The unintended consequences of this "rule" could have been anticipated if the department head had understood that differences in power matter and that quiet does not always equate with contentment. While it's good practice to encourage people in a dispute to talk with each other directly to seek informal resolution before taking more serious steps, such conversations are not always feasible. This is an example in which a power difference distorts what would otherwise be a sensible approach of trying to get disputants to resolve their problems through conversation, not confrontation.

Process Is Your Friend

So, you mustn't ignore warning signals, and you must be alert to indications of problems that may escalate, absent a little benevolent intervention. Balancing that, though, is the maxim not to push problems to premature escalation. It's a balance, and although some of it is acquired by experience (or temperament), it's also important to keep in mind the rule that process is your friend, and to be sure to follow every step of the process in turn. (Remember Bob Johansen from Chapter 1, and the unwanted consequences that might have flowed from less than assiduous attention to process while dealing with his case?) While you must stick with these problems and keep them moving through the steps, pushing them at breakneck speed is rarely productive. Moving more deliberately gives people time to think, and if you can keep yourself from being frantic, your methodical approach may help others calm down a bit, too. Consider the following situation.

A postdoc, Susan Bidwell, discovered that her mentor, Professor Archer, had submitted an abstract to a journal without her knowledge listing her as first author. She had reservations about the interpretation of the data in the abstract and about the omission of another researcher who had made significant contributions to the work, and to whom she and Archer had promised authorship. Bidwell faxed the journal editor withdrawing the abstract and then spoke to Archer, who reacted with outrage: he promptly faxed the editor himself, seeking to reinstate the abstract, asserting that he, as "responsible investigator," had a "duty and obligation" to interpret the data and assign authorship for work performed in his laboratory, and that both were correct as originally submitted. His faxed letter also impugned Bidwell's contributions, relegating her to the status of a technician, though he did not contest her first authorship on the two full manuscripts describing the work.

Professor Archer and Susan Bidwell had long had a troubled relationship. The head of their department knew this, and had previously negotiated an agreement between them about authorship. In discussion with the department head, who had been told about the dispute by the journal editor, Archer acknowledged that the agreement applied to the work described in the abstract. His view, however, was that the agreement applied only to manuscripts, not to abstracts. Further, since in his opinion there was no rule against what he'd done, only some ambiguous concepts of professional courtesy, he didn't think the matter should be of any concern to the department head. The issue of having listed Bidwell as first author while interpreting the data in a way she considered wrong was not discussed, as Archer withdrew the abstract after the department head gently, but firmly, inserted himself into the discussion.

This situation could easily have become a much larger problem had the department head not intervened. It would not have taken much to turn it into an allegation of research misconduct requiring application of formal policies and procedures: the researcher whose name was omitted could have contested the matter, as could Susan Bidwell herself. In fact, low-level disputes of this sort, especially ones in which personal relationships are strained or become so, underlie many misconduct cases that escalate into major problems.

Think about whether the department head's intervention was only necessary or was also sufficient. Does anything in the situation indicate a need for additional action by the department head, or is the satisfaction of the parties, and their willingness to declare victory and leave the field, enough to close it all out?

The answer, as in so many administrative dilemmas, is "It depends." One point worth pondering is whether this is an isolated instance of bad personal chemistry between Professor Archer and Susan Bidwell, or whether Archer's career has involved any pattern of disputes about authorship or corner-cutting on agreements. In the real-life case on which I based this scenario, the professor had a history of effective, strong collaborations, and the postdoc had a good record at other places. The department head, upon reflection and review of his files, concluded that the data were sufficiently complex and nuanced that significant differences in interpretation were plausible, and that such differences, plus the long-troubled personal relationship between the two principals, were probably at the root of the matter. He let it rest, and no further warning signals have emerged (as far as I know) since then.

But the department head did take reasonable precautions as he brought the dispute to closure: he wrote a formal letter to all the participants, including the journal editor, documenting the resolution and the original agreement about authorship, and he retained a copy in the department's files so there would be a record in the event of later recurrence of this or related problems.

Although it may seem counterintuitive, conducting a formal review can be in the best long-term interest of an innocent person accused of wrongdoing. I was once involved in a situation in which the person making allegations about a respected faculty member was so lacking in credibility that everyone who heard the accusations dismissed them out of hand. Against the inclinations of several administrative colleagues, I advised the faculty member to report the allegations himself and to ask to have them reviewed. The dean, who saw the proposed review as an exercise in futility, nevertheless acceded and commissioned a review committee. At the conclusion of a thorough process, the committee produced a report—with factual appendixes—exonerating the faculty member. Many "I told you so's" ensued. But then the accuser started a letter-writing campaign, sending denunciatory missives to every member of the faculty member's disciplinary society, every member of the state legislature, the state's congressional delegation, the governor . . .

Fortunately, the university, because it had conducted an arm's-length investigation complete with documentation, was in a position to defend the faculty member by demonstrating that there had been a thorough investigation (the faculty member waived his privacy rights on this); that the committee, the dean, the provost, and the chancellor had reviewed the report; that copies had been sent to funding agencies; and that the university had concluded that there had not been any improprieties in the situation. As a result, the faculty member's reputation did not suffer, and in fact he garnered a fair amount of sympathy from his colleagues for having been a victim of irrational persecution. Without the thorough process—conducted in its entirety by the university—the vigorous defense could not have been mounted. It's quite likely that rumors would have dogged the faculty member throughout his career, and that some people would have assumed there was fire to go with the smoke. Not only can policies and procedures be your friend when you are in charge of the process, they can be your friend when you're the target, too.

Moderate the Emotional Pitch

While relying on process, you'll also want to pay careful attention to the emotional pitch of the involved parties. Even in an informal mediation or intervention effort, allowing emotions to trump facts will, generally, exacerbate rather than improve problems. And, in any dispute, there will be a lot of emotion. Graduate students and other junior personnel will be worried that voicing concerns may have a negative effect on their careers. Senior personnel about whom concerns are expressed are likely to be quite angry that the questions were raised. All will be worried about what the process will entail, how long it will take, and what will happen to them afterward.

As you prepare to try to resolve a problem informally, the starting place is to find a way to be calm and centered. Prepare well; think through what needs to happen, and in what order. What are the items to be addressed, and who should speak first? If you can, arrange for equal numbers of people on each side of the matter to be present. If there are going to be two faculty members, for example, and one graduate student, try to get another faculty member to accompany the graduate student and serve as an advisor throughout the process. Review your listening skills, and assume your persona as the authority figure. You should be clearly in control of the discussion. Maintain a formal demeanor. Have a written agenda, and begin by setting the ground rules. Introduce the participants, the purpose of the meeting, and the time limit. Keep the discussion orderly and be sure it follows your agenda. If relevant items that are not on your agenda are raised, assign them a place on the agenda and defer them until the appropriate time. Speak more slowly and more quietly than usual. (This is a subtle and often unnoticed technique, and it will make a significant contribution to moderating the pitch.) Stop anyone who makes an insulting or offensive remark and ask that it be rephrased to focus on the issue and not the personalities in the room. Call a recess, if necessary, for people to calm down. After discussion of an item is concluded, summarize the agreement and indicate that you will include that summary in your minutes of the meeting. The more formal control you exert over the meeting, the less likely it will be to escalate into a shouting match. If you feel it spinning out, adjourn and seek guidance from a resource person on campus as to how to proceed. Consider invoking a formal procedure to add even more boundaries to the process.

Emotions often distort people's memories. For this reason, along with the many others we've discussed, it is important to keep careful records about conversations and meetings, their participants, and the topics discussed. (Remember the material on complaints in Chapter 4?)

Judge by Facts, Not Personalities

On the subject of emotions, there is a crucial point to bear in mind about your own: don't let yourself base decisions on personalities rather than facts. We all like some people better than others, and we all find it much too easy to start assessing a situation on the basis of demeanor and position rather than facts. When we are in positions of authority we have to distance ourselves from our personal reactions in the interest of fairness.

Any person caught up in a situation involving allegations of misconduct—whether as the one reporting a concern or as the accused—is unlikely to appear organized or collected when initially interviewed. Second thoughts are common. It is important to let the people interviewed know that they'll be allowed to provide additional information or ask questions later, but it is also important that you not find yourself spending all your time meeting with these people or talking with them on the telephone. Sometimes encouraging such people to seek counsel from trusted supporters or friends can be helpful—if they can discuss matters with someone (other than you) who is not emotionally involved, they may gain perspective on the situation. The key is to explain the process and your role in it clearly; repeat the explanation often and stay within the limits of your prescribed role. Be friendly and cordial to all parties, but do not become a friend or confidant.

Expressions of personal support or concern for individuals in obvious pain must be carefully stated. You do not want those expressions to be taken as evidence that you are accepting their version of the facts. Repeated statements of your neutrality and your commitment to a fair and just outcome can help ameliorate this effect.

You may have detected a theme in many of the case studies in this book: complainants who seem distraught, or less than credible, or biased, or malicious. It's one of the realities of the world that a person who comes forward about a serious problem—even one who later on, with hindsight, will be praised as a whistleblower—often appears to be a nutcase or a malcontent. As a society, we don't like children who are tattletales, and we like this conduct even less in adults. People with complaints, especially those who are at the bottom of the power curve, are all too aware of this, and also all too aware of the price that whistleblowers usually pay. It's a very stressful thing to pursue a complaint against a powerful person, and it takes a toll. Probably it also takes a special personality type. It's hard to say how all these factors interact. Nonetheless, basing your response upon your impression of that person, rather than upon an assessment of the facts involved, can lead you and your institution very far astray.

At my university, a federal criminal investigator once arrived on campus to investigate an allegation against a faculty member, which had been received directly by his agency. In the space of about a month or two, he cleared the whole thing up, found there were no problems, and went away. The faculty member sought advice about how to have him reprimanded for investigating her instead of the motives of the whistleblower, whom she considered embittered and malicious.

This illustrates the importance of looking at facts, not personalities. The investigator's job was to determine whether the allegation had any basis to it, regardless of the motive of the person who made it. The one who makes a complaint can be the most malicious, naive, or uninformed person in the world, but if the things he or she is reporting are true, *motive is irrelevant*. Very often, soon after someone raises a concern, others will question his or her motives and stability. What matters is the essential facts of the situation; letting yourself be distracted by questions about personalities is counterproductive. It's your job to keep your eye on the real issue, which is your obligation to determine what the facts are.

Know When to Call for Outside Help

When suspicions of misconduct arise, it's tempting to keep them within the department or the institution. These problems are messy, nasty, and distasteful—not the sort of news we want the outside world to hear. In many instances, there are complexities that pull in two directions at once: when there are allegations of shenanigans in highly technical research, "insiders" (whether inside your university or within the same research community) are often best situated to assess the charges; but insiders also have conflicts of interest that must be straightforwardly acknowledged and addressed before an unbiased judging process is possible. My experience is that virtually all people of sufficient professional standing to serve on a misconduct-investigation committee do see the larger principles at stake and can do the right thing—if, at the beginning of the process, the issues of integrity are articulated. Without that, it's all too easy for conflicts of interest to have a pernicious effect.

No one has a greater stake in the integrity of the institution than those of us whose professional reputations are connected to it. If the hard questions are properly presented, we can judge our own and do it well. In matters that impinge upon the central, distinctive aspects of our institutions, such as questions of research and those involving fundamental values like academic freedom and tenure, we can and do rise to the occasion. But in matters that are not unique to our settings, and for which we do not have special qualifications, the nature of the complaint may mean that outsiders are required. Let's consider another case of personalities, in this case an ugly accusation against a well-liked member of the department.

> Joe Student works for your department as a graduate assistant
> doing computer support. Max Manager supervises Joe and

thirteen others. Max is a long-term staff member, much liked and trusted. Another employee tells you she heard Max and Joe discussing what sounded like an arrangement to split the proceeds from selling some equipment off campus. She says that Max asked Joe to pick up a delivery of computer equipment (value $2,500). This equipment was logged in as received but later reported lost or stolen. You remember the incident; at the time, you had the police come in to review your security. The reporting employee, who wishes to remain anonymous, says she suspects that the same sort of thing has happened before. You know and like Max, and you also know that the reporting employee is jealous of his position in the department and his popularity. What should you do?

Does this situation sound implausible to you? Unfortunately, it happens all the time. This is an example of an allegation that, if it's true, is very serious, and you must handle it accordingly from the very beginning. No matter how sure you are that you could resolve this problem by talking to Max quietly, you should not take that approach in this circumstance. Taking things that don't belong to you is called stealing. It's a serious boundary violation that damages the community. The people who deal with stealing are the police. Because this situation involves an allegation of a criminal offense— even if you hope and believe it to be untrue—you must report it immediately to whatever police department has jurisdiction over your university (and possibly to your institution's lawyers as well). If your institution has its own police force, this hard step may be a bit easier, as you'll have less fear of letting outsiders know about a potentially unfounded allegation.

Of course you don't like to believe the worst of someone, especially someone you work with on a regular basis and feel you know well. And of course you'd rather not become known as the head of a unit in which criminal activity is rampant. All too frequently, organizations sweep incidents like the accusation of Max and Joe under the rug, letting people resign quietly if the allegations turn out to be true, or even just dismissing the allegations as sour grapes. That way of handling the situation is not in the best interests of the larger institution. Nor does it send the right message to those who know about it or later learn about it—and you can be sure that it will be known about and discussed in your department and elsewhere.

Imagine for a moment what could happen if you decide to ignore the employee's accusation on the assumption that it arose out of her unreasonable jealousy of Max. If she is convinced that Max and others are stealing, she may eventually take her information to others, such as the internal auditors or local newspapers. If public funds were involved in the purchase of the missing equipment, there's a larger issue of stewardship. Not to mention that if the allegation is true, overlooking it means that the thefts are likely to continue. Whether the report is a malicious lie or whether it turns out to be accurate, this is not the kind of situation that will go away if ignored.

Serious allegations must be reviewed with a level of formality—either to confirm or to debunk them. In the case of an alleged criminal offense like stealing, the police will do whatever investigation is necessary, and will bring some closure to the matter. If the allegation is substantiated, they must be allowed to handle it according to prescribed procedures. If it is not substantiated, the fact that they have investigated and cleared Max and Joe will prevent your jealous employee—who will have experienced some "blue therapy" herself by being interviewed in the course of the investigation—from continuing to make the accusation.

Will Max and Joe and the would-be anonymous reporter be happy with you at the end of the process? Probably not. Can you afford not to pursue such a situation? Absolutely not. Your responsibility to look out for the good of the whole demands that you act. And know what? While you may fear looking bad because this happened on your watch, in fact you'll look better for responding forthrightly and promptly. No stain will attach to your reputation the way that it will if you ignore the problem and it mushrooms or your nonresponse is seen as quiet collusion. Even if the situation becomes public and messy (well, messier), your plight will generate empathy and positive regard because you've done the hard, right thing.

Anonymous Allegations, Reprised

Concerns regarding academic conduct can come from a variety of sources. Sometimes students or faculty with first-hand knowledge of practices that may be improper come to see you; some complaints are conveyed second-hand. Allegations span a spectrum from apparently insubstantial to obviously quite serious. The first response to expressions of concern can be crucial to the outcome for all the individuals involved and for the institution. Because people expressing such concerns are often upset, angry, and frightened, it can be difficult during an initial interview to determine whether or not they are alleging misconduct. More often than not, the concerns raised are not about academic misconduct, but other issues, like miscommunication or insensitivity, that require a response but are not (thankfully) as serious or as potentially damaging as allegations of misconduct. This is not to say you can ignore the concerns, but only that they will usually be comparatively easy to handle.

In the case of Max Manager, the allegation was made by someone known to you, though she wanted to remain anonymous. At other times reports may come to you completely anonymously. As tempting as it is, an anonymous allegation of wrongdoing often should not (and frequently cannot—remember the legal concept of being placed "on notice") be ignored, but it is also important not to embark upon what could be perceived as a witch hunt purely on the basis of unverified statements by unknown persons.

Clearly there is a difference between poison-pen letters slipped under the door and statements made by an identifiable person who is afraid of possible retaliation. If the allegations involve facts that can be independently verified, the situation is different from one that depends upon the credibility or interpretation of the (anonymous) informant. In the former circumstance, it may be possible to be fair to the accused person (by providing full notice and opportunity to respond) while still protecting the individual who raised the concern. In the latter, it is probably not. Further, it is unwise to promise anonymity for the duration of the process. Anonymity is difficult to protect on a practical level, and becomes increasingly troubling from the perspective of fairness as the process proceeds.

Formal versus Informal Process

Often, by the time a person comes forward to express concerns about someone's conduct, the situation is already quite complex from an interpersonal perspective. The concerns may range from issues of scientific integrity to sloppiness to sexual misconduct to exploitation of students. Most institutions have separate policies for research misconduct, financial finagling, sexual misconduct, and other such areas. At this initial stage, the safest advice is: the more complex the matter, the more likely it is to need to be handled within formal procedures. Go back and review the advice on complaints in Chapter 4, and remember: when in doubt, go formal. Formal procedure gives everyone involved much more protection, even and especially, counterintuitively, when the charges are false.

These issues are not easy to deal with, but the way you approach them will make an enormous difference—not only for you but for those in your department and, if it's not too overblown to say it this way, for the integrity of our entire system. The idea is for you to stay centered and balanced so you can help everyone navigate a difficult situation in the most constructive way possible. Keep the big picture in mind, and understand that there will probably be some painful moments. Even if you extend yourself to the maximum degree to respect the dignity (and the presumed innocence) of all concerned, there are going to be aspects of these situations that are just plain uncomfortable. Try to see them in context. Persevere. And then, go home and take care of yourself.

Chapter 8

Centering

As word spreads about your new position as head of the department at Big U, you begin receiving email from colleagues around the country, forwarding material that a member of your department, Professor Dart, has been sending out via email and electronic discussion groups on the topic "Corruption and Politics as Usual at Big U." These missives complain about the process used for your appointment, although the writer is careful to state that he has nothing personally against you, and that as far as he knows you may be a person of integrity. Others in the department also write to you, saying that they are looking forward to your service and welcoming you to the role. Several mention that they believe something needs to be done about the department's black eye.

When our children were small, my husband and I were puzzled whenever someone told us we were lucky that they were so polite. As far as we could tell, our children had neither been born with the politeness gene activated nor been visited by fairy godmothers who sprinkled them with politeness dust. There were days when we thought we were probably the only parents on the planet who spent every waking minute trying to graft a thin veneer of manners onto our forthright offspring. We didn't feel lucky, we felt tired. It was, of course, gratifying that people saw positive things about our children, but it seemed odd to label their politeness a matter of "luck" and not hard work.

If your department has an atmosphere of civility, if its denizens observe reasonable boundaries and are able to devote most of their time to productive endeavors rather than internecine warfare, you, too, may be told you are "lucky." And, in fact, there is an element of luck in the chemistry of any group. We've all had classes with great group personalities and classes that, no matter what we try, have an attitude that makes teaching them seem like pushing boulders uphill, for no discernible reason other than the way the group jelled, or didn't. But beyond the basic mix, if your department is harmonious and a good place to work, it is more than likely that someone has put in a great deal of effort behind the scenes, whether that someone is you or some set of your predecessors. Whether consciously and strategically or simply by instinct, someone worked to create an atmosphere of respect for all members of the department, from the lowest-ranking, lowest-paid support staff member to the brightest superstar.

Never underestimate how much effort it takes to establish and maintain such an environment. If you've inherited it, don't get complacent and think you can devote all your energy to other areas. The effect of entropy is such that, without careful tending, boundaries will be pushed, advantage will be taken, weight will be thrown around, and the environment will deteriorate.

The best way to maintain a good environment is to have a strong conceptual model of what your role is and a full bag of techniques and strategies available for trying to build and maintain it. We've discussed various aspects of those items. There are two more concepts for you to consider as we bring this survival guide to a close.

Likeability Matters

The first concept, from the negotiation literature, boils down to this: likeability matters. If you think about it, this makes perfect sense. It's easier to do things for people you like than for those you see as rude or nasty. Remember the grandmotherly wisdom I cited in Chapter 3: you catch more flies with honey than with vinegar. Do you know someone who leaves you smiling after every interaction? How motivated are you to find ways to make things work for that person? Now, compare that with your feelings about someone whose exchanges with you are always contentious. How strong is your motivation to help that person? These are qualitatively different experiences.

This works in both directions. Just as you respond more positively to people you like, in group life, where you interact with the same people over and over, the more pleasant you are, the more positively people will respond to you. In a positive frame of mind, they will be more likely to listen to your point of view, carefully consider what you say, and pause before escalating any disagreement into unpleasantness. In contrast, the more you tend to be rude and cutting in interactions, the more you will find the rudeness reciprocated. How many people do you know who have actually been persuaded by insults and invective? When was the last time you heard someone respond to being called stupid by saying "Oh, you're right, thanks"?

People don't always realize how they are affecting others. I worked for years with a man who was terse and unfriendly, especially in email. He thought of himself as a warm, teddy-bear kind of fellow who simply saved time by "cutting to the chase," and he appeared to have no idea that those around him perceived him as so mean-spirited that they avoided him as much as possible. Over and over, interactions with him turned into shouting matches: he saw his colleagues as difficult and contentious, not recognizing his own contributions to the frequent combative exchanges. I, too, found him exceedingly disagreeable, but by being relentlessly cheerful and pleasant to him—by treating him as if he were the teddy bear he thought he was—I managed to elicit similar behavior from him. In other words, you reap what you sow.

Being likeable is not the same as having low standards for quality, a lesson that seems lost on some people in academia. And being unpleasant is certainly not evidence that you have high standards. In fact, making sincerely felt positive comments can reduce defensiveness and help you introduce change to raise standards or bring improvements. Thus likeability is a skill that will help you get the job done.

The Persona Pendulum

The other concept to consider is related to the idea, discussed earlier in this book, that you may need a special persona for your leadership responsibilities. By now you surely understand that you can be friendly, but not friends, when you are responsible for evaluating and supervising others. There's another wrinkle, though: your job demands that you purposefully alter your relationships with members of your department depending upon where they are in their careers. This swinging back and forth like a pendulum can be disorienting, and it can be hard both for you and for those you are supervising, especially if you have not thought it through with some care in advance. This aspect goes back to which "you" you should be in any given circumstance, and at its heart are the boundary issues you must internalize to succeed as an administrator.

Think about what you do when recruiting someone to join your department, whether as a faculty member, a grad student, or an administrative professional. Recruiting is a form of seduction: you're selling yourself, your department, your university, and your community. You are saying "Imagine yourself productive and happy in our department. Here's what we can do for you (salary, working conditions, lab space, colleagues, opportunity to grow, and so on), and here's how you'll fit in and the contribution you'll make here. See the pretty picture? Your whole life here will be good. The work will be challenging and interesting with great colleagues, and we'll help you find a house and good schools for your current or future children, and we'll hook you up with like-minded people in the community, whatever your interests may be." In flat central Illinois, when we recruit people (especially those from places with flashier scenery or balmier climates), we dwell on the virtues of our community for raising a family and the support our university provides for people to do their best work with a low hassle factor.

Once your target makes the decision to join your department, you switch from recruiting mode to a mentoring/cheerleading phase in which you help her get established and learn to feel at home. You express confidence, provide advice, and generally encourage the newcomer. This stage is focused on the needs of the recruit, with you doing all you can to support her success.

Before long, though, you have to switch personas again, this time to the role of objective evaluator. Whether this is a three- or six-month review for a probationary secretary, an annual evaluation, or the all-important third-year review or even tenure decision for a faculty member, it's time for you to assess the employee's progress. Note that you are now acting entirely in a supervisory, evaluative role. While you can remain friendly, your first obligation is to provide an assessment of the person's job performance—still aimed at supporting success, but now in terms of the university's standards and goals. (I'll have more to say about this stage in the next section.)

Right after you've done this hard thing, providing a clear and objective evaluation, you'll switch back to your cheerleading persona until it's once again time to make the "up or out" choice: promotion, tenure, passing the prelims, or moving off probationary status. Yes, you may feel like a pendulum, swinging from one role to another and back again at set intervals—and yet you must try to remain centered through it all.

Balance and Clarity

Switching gears from cheerleading to firm-but-fair assessment that includes analysis and description of deficits in performance as well as strengths can be very difficult. You may respond to the difficulty by pulling your punches, especially if you have developed a genuine liking for the person you must now evaluate. This is not a helpful response. For the same reasons we discussed earlier about the importance of making your expectations clear when things are not going well with an employee, it is essential that you be clear and direct in both your positive and your negative assessments.

We know from social psychology that humans are prone to biased and self-serving assimilation of information, which means that the person you are assessing is much more likely to hear your positive comments than your negative ones. Especially because you've so recently been in a mentoring/cheerleading role, he will be likely to discount any but the clearest statements of any shortcomings in his job performance. (A useful book for understanding this and related phenomena is *How We Know What Isn't So* by Thomas Gilovich.)

In an illuminating psychology experiment, fans of two rival teams watching a game tape saw dramatically different qualities of officiating, depending upon which team they were rooting for. In another, lawyers or law students assigned to assess the monetary value of a case from identical facts or case descriptions came up with very different numbers, depending on whether they were told they were representing one side or the other or acting as a neutral judge. All of us key in on facts in our favor and tend to pay less attention to the ones that are less positive for our side. Most of the people you evaluate will do the same thing: they'll see better, remember more clearly, and focus more strongly upon the encouragement that says they're doing well; and they may not take in the caveats, particularly if they are too gently or diplomatically phrased.

You may encounter some people who have the opposite tendency: to overreact and go off the deep end at even a hint of criticism. This reaction is rooted in the insecure overachieving personality we've discussed before. It also carries an element of emotional blackmail, so you'll need to be especially balanced and evenhanded with those personalities. Don't go overboard in your attempts to provide reassurance, or, thanks to the self-serving bias, your listener may take away the message that all is well after all.

Whatever personality type you're dealing with, it is up to you to

provide an evenhanded assessment and to communicate it clearly—
and in writing. If an assistant professor is spending too much time
on teaching or service and not making enough progress in building
a publication record, each and every written evaluation must say so.
Your mantra should be "no surprises." So when it comes time for
the tenure evaluation or the termination of the contract because of
insufficient publication, a retrospective look through every evaluation should show a clear development of straightforward warnings
about what was needed and the progress being made each time.

Far too often, department heads and supervisors think they are
doing someone a favor when they soften bad news by embedding
it in encouragement. Remember the maxim that no good deed
goes unpunished. Of course you want to encourage the people in
your department. But that worthy impulse carries a danger: if you
work too hard to soften bad news, you may fail to communicate it
at all. And then, when the story plays out, because the person does
not make the changes that are needed to get back on track, the outcome will be an unpleasant surprise. And guess who will be seen as
the bad guy, instead of as someone doing a favor?

Do not set yourself up to become the target of disappointment
and anger when the final bad news is communicated. Think of
the "third reader" discussed in Chapter 6, the outsider who assesses
the situation without knowing the participants. When your disappointed employee shows her evaluation record to someone else
(whether just for commiseration or preparatory to filing a complaint or lawsuit), you want that third reader to say "But your department head has been telling you each and every year that you
were not making good progress."

Be specific. Consider the difference between the following two
evaluations:

> Your publication record needs to be enhanced, and we are confident you can do it.
>
> We understand there has been a significant set-up period for your work. To stay on track, you now need to focus strongly on getting your work published, so that by your next evaluation you will have had manuscripts published or accepted for publication in the outlets we have discussed that will help establish your reputation.

Or, for a staff member, consider the difference between these two:

> More accuracy and timeliness would be good, and we see you making progress toward those.
>
> As we have discussed, the frequent errors in and late submissions of the budget reports for which you are responsible are a problem. The budget reports must be accurate, complete, and submitted on time each period, so that they are routinely signed off on by the college office and not returned to us for correction and modification. If you feel more training would help you meet this goal, or if you feel there are problems of which I am not aware that are preventing you from meeting it, it is your responsibility to bring this to my attention no later than Friday, [date].

If you were the person being evaluated, which type of wording would be most helpful to you? And if you were the third reader consulted by an employee unhappy about not being promoted, in which wording would you see more grounds for appealing the determination or filing a grievance or a lawsuit?

Another aspect of academic life may also be disorienting: the fact that faculty members typically have two different pipers to dance to—the internal community of the university and the external community of colleagues in their discipline. Of course, you think, everyone knows this, it's a no-brainer. But the problem is, just as fish forget about the water they swim in, you may well lose sight of the effects of this arrangement on faculty members' motivation. For example, since major rewards such as grants and professional recognition come primarily from their external audience (and since even the all-important tenure decision depends heavily on assessments provided by outside scholars), their reasons to pay attention to the internal audience may be diminished. This creates a very real tension that you should confront and discuss with every faculty member for whom you have assessment responsibilities—especially those just starting out. Being aware of the "two pipers" will help you guide your faculty, particularly the younger members, to maintain a balance between the two sets of colleagues.

Our old friend Janus exemplifies this situation well, I think. He is depicted with two faces looking in opposite directions, and this is what it sometimes feels as if faculty members have to do. If you're not clear about this Janus-like responsibility, how can you expect the faculty to be?

Outside the university, each faculty member's field or discipline sets professional norms, while the university's internal regulations and culture, both within a department and across the institution, also set expectations for and govern conduct. Membership in good professional standing must be maintained in both institutional and intellectual communities for an individual's career to prosper. While research universities are at least implicitly aware of these overlapping responsibilities, a somewhat sharper understanding is also required. Before questions arise, you should be clear about the order of precedence and priority between internal and external standards if and when they come into conflict. If you have not considered these potential conflicts, start thinking about them now.

I once was involved in a case in which an engineering professor was alleged to be publishing the same work (without cross-references) in multiple outlets. His response was that "of course" he did that, since in engineering, practitioners and theoreticians have different outlets and multiple publication is seen as helpful. He asserted that he was fulfilling an obligation to reach as many members of his profession as possible. His university's policy used as an ethical standard "practices commonly accepted within the professional community." The reviewing committee raised the question of which professional community was meant: the university's, or that of the engineering profession? The answer was that university standards applied to all university faculty members, but the question was asked in great seriousness, as it should have been. If your faculty members aren't clear about what their professional responsibilities and ethical codes are, it's your job to rectify that.

Professor Dart's Complaints

It's likely that your peers across the country and in your own institution are talking about the emails attributing your appointment to "politics and corruption," and that they are watching to see how you will react. Your response will say important things about you.

First, know thyself: What *is* your reaction? Do the notes embarrass you? Make you cringe? Make you angry? Make you laugh? Cause you concern for the colleague who is writing them? What kind of concern? Why?

If you take the criticism or complaint personally, you're far more likely to overreact, be defensive, or otherwise respond in an uncon-structive way. The ability to accept criticism with openness and to acknowledge the critic's feelings, without getting personal, is a far more effective way to keep friends and influence people. (Okay. Even if you accept all the reasons not to take things personally, there are going to be some situations that hurt your feelings, and that you do take personally. The key in those situations is not to let it show.)

Inside the department, don't lash out, but also don't let Dart's be-havior go unchecked. Call it for what it is: let it be known that you are having to spend an unfortunate amount of time on this, to the detriment of the department's goals. If the time you must devote to responding to this tempest in a teacup delays your ability to re-spond to colleagues' requests for specific items, say so directly. Take a tip from studies of good parenting: let actions have their logical (but nonpunitive) consequences. If the accusations Dart is dissemi-nating are demonstrably unfounded, send him a short note docu-menting that fact and keep a copy for yourself. Keep a record of all the communications you receive from him, or from others for-warding his missives. If you stay calm, clear, and consistent, and don't push the outcome, one of two things will happen: he will wind down, or he will escalate in a way that creates a group will-ingness and a procedural basis for taking action against him. Hope for the former, but be prepared for the latter just in case.

Assuming you did nothing out of the ordinary during the search process, you are neither the target of Dart's diatribes nor responsible for the process about which he is complaining. But they are surely exposing your department to unwanted publicity and scrutiny, and people will raise the topic with you. It would be wise to prepare a response that portrays you, your department, and your institution in the best possible light. If there's anything you can do to disarm negative effects of the complaints, all the better.

What kind of response might you construct? In talking with others, one important element is to convey some sense of the integrity of the appointment process and your faith in it and the institution. (If you have such faith.) Another is to make it clear that Professor Dart has a right to his views and you're sorry he feels the way he does; you might try a rueful smile and a humorous response about the favor he's doing you by helping you thicken your skin so early in your term. If others are ridiculing Dart, it's crucial that you not participate, not make any derogatory remarks. At most, you should convey a sense of empathy for how painful he must find it to feel that the institution he's served for so long is heading down the wrong path.

In Praise of Praise

My emphasis in this chapter on being clear when delivering bad news is not meant to downplay the importance—or the strategic value—of telling people when they're doing well. It's not just the insecure overachievers among us who need praise: everyone does. Not only that, but giving sincere praise is one way of being pleasant, and as we've already discussed, if you're seen as pleasant and likeable you'll have a better chance of fostering an environment in which change is possible. People are more likely to cooperate when they feel they and their work are recognized and valued. The less attractive the venture on which you're asking them to cooperate— budget cuts, say—the more their sense of being respected will count.

This means that an overlooked secret to achieving your goals for your term of service is to learn to praise. Bear this in mind and try to make positive statements, however small, as often as they're warranted. The praise has to be plausible, it has to be related to the job (no falling back on merely complimenting new haircuts), and you have to mean it (blatant hypocrisy is easily detectable). The praise you offer needn't always be public, although a reasonable proportion of it should be. Don't praise what people are (as in "You're so smart"), but what they do, or even what they could do if they saw in themselves the potential that you see. Focus on the efforts they make that contribute to the mission of your unit. You may be surprised at how many admirable actions and traits you find when you are looking for them: from the secretary who volunteers to stay late to get a grant application out on time to the star professor who always attends the ethics seminar for graduate students to show that the faculty is committed to ethical conduct.

Prizes and awards are common in the academy, praise and encouragement, much less so. By giving praise and encouragement, you give something rare and valuable, and sometimes even memorable. And you may tacitly suggest to your colleagues that someday they might appreciate and praise you, too.

Universities are wonderful places. They are filled with smart, dedicated people. It's your job, as an administrator, to provide an environment that brings out the best in those people. If you don't, all these quirky and interesting people may find their energies diverted in ways that do not serve the mission of advancing the frontiers of knowledge and fostering the intellectual growth of generations of young men and women. While the outcome is not entirely within your control, in the small piece that is your responsibility, do what you can to leave the institution better than you found it. And step back every now and then to relish the excitement and the small victories.

For Further Reading

This is not your typical book about life in universities, so these are not the typical recommendations you're likely to find elsewhere. Give them a try. All are readily available, most in paperback.

Negotiation and Persuasion

C. Craver, *The Intelligent Negotiator: What to Say, What to Do, How to Get What You Want—Every Time* (Three Rivers Press, 2002).

W. Ury, *Getting Past No: Negotiating Your Way from Confrontation to Cooperation* (Bantam, 1993). Accessible and useful. This book is well worth revisiting from time to time for a mental tune-up about how to approach conflict and negotiation.

R. Shell, *Bargaining for Advantage: Negotiation Strategies for Reasonable People* (Penguin, 2000). An accessible, helpful book on the fundamentals of negotiation, organized first around habits of thought and preparation and then around strategies.

12 Angry Men. This extraordinary movie is a masterly example of effective persuasion in action. Watch it to learn what circumstances help people change their minds in group situations.

R. Lewicki, D. Saunders, B. Barry, and J. Minton, *Essentials of Negotiation,* 3rd edition (McGraw-Hill/Irwin, 2003). Used as a text in many negotiation courses; includes a wide range of useful readings.

Conflict and Difficult People

D. Stone, B. Patton, and S. Heen, *Difficult Conversations: How to Discuss What Matters Most* (New York: Penguin Putnam, 2000). I recommend this book more often than any other. It is equally applicable to personal and professional interactions.

G. Thompson, *Verbal Judo: The Gentle Art of Persuasion* (Quill, 2004). This popular book has some useful tips.

W. Ury, J. Brett, and S. Goldberg, *Getting Disputes Resolved* (Jossey-Bass, 1988). Presents the "interests, rights, and power" model, which is worth incorporating into your working life.

M. Deutsch and P. Coleman, *The Handbook of Conflict Resolution: Theory and Practice* (Jossey-Bass, 2000). Worth browsing, especially at a time when you're not embroiled in conflict, to advance your thinking on conflict and its resolution.

Influencing People

R. Cialdini, *Influence: Science and Practice* (Collins, 1998). A great primer on what social psychology has revealed about influencing people, for those outside the field.

C. Dweck, *Mindset: The New Psychology of Success* (Random House, 2006). Dweck's research on motivation is useful for anyone who supervises or teaches others.

S. Plous, *The Psychology of Judgment and Decision Making* (McGraw-Hill, 1993). Another primer summarizing key findings in social psychology.

T. Gilovich, *How We Know What Isn't So: The Fallibility of Human Reason in Everyday Life* (Free Press, 1993). Especially valuable in the context of university life, where we all like to think we're basing our actions on reason.

Management in General

W. Oncken and D. Wass, "Management Time: Who's Got the Monkey?" *Harvard Business Review,* November 1999. A classic article. Only six pages long, it has valuable concepts about problem-solving, delegation, and "being the boss."

A. Faber and E. Mazlish, *How to Talk So Kids Will Listen and Listen So Kids Will Talk* (Avon, 1980). One of my favorite parenting books. Topics like sibling rivalry turn out to be highly relevant to life in university departments.

C. Cherry, *Parents, Please Don't Sit on Your Kids: A Parent's Guide to Non-Punitive Discipline* (Fearon Teaching Aids, 1996). A clear and helpful explanation of nonpunitive discipline. The mind-set is exactly what all the negotiation books are trying to teach.

R. Dreikurs, *Children: The Challenge* (Penguin Plume, 1990). A more academic work.

P. McConnell, *The Other End of the Leash* (Ballantine, 2002); and K. Pryor, *Don't Shoot the Dog! The New Art of Teaching and Training* (Bantam, 1999). These books are applied behavioral psychology. If you grasp the principles in one setting (often easier when it's not your own), you'll be able to apply them in others.

F. Reichheld, *The Loyalty Effect: The Hidden Force behind Growth, Profits, and Hidden Value* (Harvard Business School Press, 2001). If the business orientation doesn't put you off, there's much food for thought here.

J. Pfeffer and R. Sutton, *The Knowing-Doing Gap: How Smart Companies Turn Knowledge into Action* (Harvard Business School Press, 2000). This may seem far afield from being responsible for a unit in a university, but it provides an interesting perspective worth considering, if you have some time to read outside your field.

Handling Misconduct

American Association for the Advancement of Science, *Responding to Allegations of Research Misconduct: Inquiry and Investigation, A Practicum* (AAAS, 1997).

Universities and How They Work

H. Rosovsky, *The University: An Owner's Manual* (Norton, 1990). The chapter "A Dean's Day" is especially revealing. Don't read it if you haven't already accepted your position. Do read it after you've taken the job.

Credits

Portions of Chapter 4 are based on my articles "How to Blow the Whistle and Still Have a Career Afterwards" and "Preventing the Need for Whistleblowing: Practical Advice for University Administrators," which appeared in *Science and Engineering Ethics* 4 (1998). I am grateful for permission to use the material here, as well as for permission from the University of Illinois to include passages adapted from case studies and training materials I developed while working in campus administration.

Acknowledgments

One of the privileges of working in a large organization is that there are so many people from whom to learn. I have been fortunate in my colleagues, mentors, teachers, and friends at the University of Illinois. Over time, my network of teachers and friends has grown to include people at other institutions as well. I owe all of those with whom I have worked a debt of gratitude, especially for bearing with me while I was growing up as a professional and learning many of the lessons described in this book, some of them quite painfully.

Don Bitzer was the first person who invested in my career. He gave me unprecedented opportunities, starting when I was just sixteen years old. In the decade that followed, I had the privilege of working in an organization Don led—and it was led, not managed. In my years at the PLATO lab, I was able to earn two degrees, try my hand at disparate tasks, rub shoulders with many highly and variously talented people, gain my first introduction to legal issues and university administration, learn that I was not meant to be a computer programmer, and discover that I was a pretty fair organizer. I also got married and had my first child. Through that decade of change and growth, Don provided inspiration and profound lessons in leadership.

Dillon Mapother gave me my next opportunity. He and Sharon Tipsword showed me how to balance precision with effectiveness in an administrative office. I owe them both a great deal. Ted

Brown, the vice chancellor for research in that era, taught me by example about compassionate leadership.

During that part of my career, I met Judy Rowan and Steve Veazie, who have been shaping influences ever since. It would be hard to overestimate or precisely describe how much they have taught me and how much their friendship has meant to me. How many years did it take you, Steve, to drum into me that "less can be more" in problem situations?

Knowing Judy has been life-changing. Among her many gifts to me was her introduction to Tom Everhart, the next mentor who gave me wonderful and unexpected opportunities. While in his office, I began working with chancellors and vice chancellors and their staffs, my colleagues for most of the next twenty years. Each had important lessons to impart. I am especially indebted to Ned Goldwasser for his faith in me. Tom, Ned, Judith Liebman, Bob Berdahl, Mort Weir, and Michael Aiken oversaw my career in "yucky problems" and supported me through a long period of difficulties that we all worked through together. Their commitment to institutional integrity was always central to their decisions.

What can I say about Paula Hays, who entered my life as a student employee in my office in that era and has been a friend and colleague ever since? Growing with Paula has been a joy. Her wisdom has taught me much.

Working for Larry Faulkner and with Nancy McCowen was one of the real privileges of my career. Their intellect and humanity shaped their decisions and continue to influence mine. Nancy was a true partner in a variety of endeavors, and to this day I miss that partnership. Her experience and wisdom guide me constantly in my approaches to dealing with people and problems. Larry gave me a standard by which to measure those to whom I give my professional loyalty and effort. It's the gold standard. With Larry and Nancy's constant support, I worked with colleagues across campus to build networks and systems, revise policies, and buttress institutional integrity and decisionmaking. We were always guided by the question Larry invariably asked: "What's in the best interest of the institution?"

The confederation of problem-solvers in those days was challenging, rigorous, caring, and efficient. Nancy's lessons, and those of Harriett Weatherford and "the View from Tuscola," became the foundations of all I know about working with and managing people. Kris Fitzpatrick was central to my learning, with her calm and uncomplaining tutoring in the world of policing with purpose, as was seeing how Paul Joffe's diagnostic skills and care for all employees and students could assist in complex situations. Mary Ellen O'Shaughnessy and I share the bond of losing our mothers too early in life, her verve enriches my life—and she has taught me much about patience. Deb Kincaid's unfailing goodwill, good cheer, and strong work ethic kept all the projects coordinated and made them go as smoothly as possible. Dick Wheeler, Elyne Cole, Bob Foertsch, Carol Livingstone, Shirley Apperson, Karen Carney, Lamar Murphy, Pam Hohn, Carol Kirkpatrick, Bill Riley, Melanie Loots, Anthony Walesby, Mike Owen, Matt Jones, Bob Damrau, Franci Miller—the list of the talented and dedicated people I was fortunate enough to collaborate with and learn from is long.

Jill Kagle started as a colleague, became a friend, and has come to be a surrogate mother to me. Love to you, Jill.

And then there are all the department heads, deans, and other university administrators who not only educated me but honored me with their trust. People who were particularly generous to me include Hassan Aref, Phil Best, Paul Bohn, Sharon Bryan, Dave

Daniel, Fred Delcomyn, Manny Donchin, Pete Feuille, Martha Gillette, Bill Greenough, Mildred Griggs, Bill Hall, John Hedeman, Jack Kamerer, Dave Kuck, Sarah Mangelsdorf, Kent Monroe, Elaine Nicholas, Dick Schacht, Alex Scheeline, Brad Schwartz, Ed Shoben, Olga Soffer, David Swanson, Hank Taylor, Mur Taylor, and Ted Valli. Matt Finkin has been a superb tutor about applications of academic freedom through the years (any mistakes in this area, though, are my own) and has saved me from missteps more than once. I owe much to Tom Mengler, for whom I worked when he was interim provost and then again when I moved to the law school. Finally, my admiration for Kathleen Conlin knows no bounds; her creativity and principled problem-solving show how it can all come together in practice.

This appreciation for special people wouldn't be complete without a mention of Jesse Delia. As department head, dean, and provost, Jesse's depth of vision and wisdom about higher education and its inhabitants is part of what has shaped the University of Illinois in which I believe so deeply.

Carol Robison's friendship, her safeguarding of versions of the manuscript, as well as her constant willingness to help in many other ways and her precision have been much appreciated. The welcome from my new colleagues at the College of Law has been helpful and important for me. Thanks especially to Andy Leipold, Dick Kaplan, and Nina Tarr for their warmth and support. Greg Northcraft was generous beyond reason when I started to teach negotiation, sharing his wisdom, experience, materials, time, and advice. My most recent teaching partnership with Steve Beckett has given me new energy and direction. Thanks, Steve.

I owe much to my supporters while this book was being written. Ken Tolo has been a friend since our first supercomputer meeting many, many years ago. Bob Secor and Russ Snyder encouraged me and convinced me that there were things we had learned at Illinois that would be helpful to others, a point that was later reinforced by Lynne Hellmer. Joe Zolner gave me the privilege of working with the wonderful groups in the Harvard Management Development Program that he has shaped and guided with such acumen over many years. Horace Freeland Judson first suggested I write a book and has been generous with his wisdom. Joyce Hudson has been a support through thick and thin. Lisa Huson read and commented on the manuscript—thank you, friend! Deb Aronson helped to tighten the manuscript and its structure. Becky McCabe read several chapters and gave me useful feedback. I've learned from watching Gene Amberg's many years of principled and caring leadership of the Urbana School District and am proud to know him.

The good fortune of meeting a wonderful editor with vision and patience cannot be overstated, nor overvalued. Elizabeth Knoll coaxed this project along through two different incarnations. Her belief in the project and in me is what made it all come together. Thank you, Elizabeth. And thank you, Drummond Rennie, for introducing me to Elizabeth, among all the other gifts of knowing you.

And then there's my family: Jovanna Stanley read and commented on several versions of the manuscript; I'm lucky she came into my life. Nancy Delcomyn has been like a sister to me for decades, and knowing the Delcomyns as a family has been a pleasure and a privilege. Of course, the fact that I grew up as one of seven children in a complicated family, most of whom became scientists, was a powerful influence. Certainly, many of the lessons recounted here were shaped by my father's academic and scientific career.

My daughters, Kearney and Anna Shea, are the lights of my life and have taught me many of the lessons that appear in this book. They surface here in many forms, not least of which is the concept of "another later." Kearney read and commented on the manuscript, and has always believed in me and my ability to bring this project to completion. I love you, sweetie. Anna Shea's willingness to make room for the book in our lives and her thoughtfulness and caring and—dare I say it?—patience with the project have been affirming for me. I love you, button.

And, always, Michael is the foundation on which all else in my life rests. I still cannot believe I was smart enough to choose you when I was so young and otherwise so uncertain. My life and work are what they are because of our partnership.

Index

academic freedom, 1, 1, 17, 45, 48–51, 56, 115, 124, 195, 206, 236; examples of, 48–49, 51–52, 56, 61
accusations, 134, 172, 182, 201, 206, 208. *See also* allegations
administrators, 1, 10, 16, 30, 36, 68, 72, 89, 108, 110, 143, 159, 174, 216, 225
aggression, 122, 135. *See also* verbal assault; violence
agreement, examples of, 198–200
allegations: examples of, 179, 181–182; of research misconduct, 5, 6, 173, 189, 200, 229. *See also* accusations
American Association of University Professors, 17, 48
Americans with Disabilities Act (ADA), 146, 156–158
anonymous: allegations, 141, 166–169, 209, 210; letters, 141–142, 166, 168–170
attacks, personal, 31, 135, 140
authority, arrogation of, 119–120, 136–137, 140
authority figure, 11, 19, 22, 27, 31, 36, 53, 71, 77, 98, 147, 203
authorship, 176–178, 182, 183, 188, 199–201; author, first, 185, 186, 199; coauthors, 177–179; examples of, 198–200
avoidance, 31, 126–127

behavior, 14, 18, 19, 25, 28, 31, 32, 37, 48, 49, 52, 56, 61, 69–72, 121, 122, 127–130, 133, 134, 176, 193
bias, personal, 151
blue therapy, 129, 130, 208; examples of, 126–129
body language, 37, 74
boundaries, 18, 19, 32–35, 38, 42, 45, 53, 71, 97–99, 102, 115, 122, 128, 132, 134–136,

213; crossing personal, 176; examples of, 44–45, 47, 51, 61, 63–65
bullies, 119, 121–125, 127, 129–131, 133, 135, 137, 139; aggressor bullies, 123–124; examples of, 119–120, 136–137, 140; victim bullies, 123–124
button-pushing, 14–16, 238

campus police, 128, 129
charges, 14, 110, 125, 151, 155, 161, 186, 202, 206, 211
classroom conduct/speech, examples of, 48–49, 51–52, 56, 61, 194–195
coauthors, 177–179. *See also* authorship
collecting information, examples of, 96–97, 115–118
collegiality, 48, 51, 52, 124, 129, 130, 139
communication, examples of, 179, 181–182. *See also* email
community, 19, 47, 50, 52, 53, 100, 122, 174, 182, 207, 216, 221–222
complaints, 7, 61, 62, 96–99, 101–103, 107, 109–111, 115–117, 119, 120, 138, 164, 172, 173, 180, 195, 196, 205, 206, 222; examples of, 44–45, 47, 51, 61, 63–65, 96–97, 115–118; handling, 99, 101, 102; legal, 102
compromises, 15, 55, 105
conduct, 14, 18, 19, 31, 49, 52, 61, 64, 70, 71, 108, 111, 119–122, 125–127, 130, 131, 134–136, 147, 148; personal, 52, 127
confidences, 45, 46, 62, 98–100, 216; examples of, 44–45, 47, 51, 61, 63–65
confidentiality, 45, 46, 110
conflict, 2, 5, 16, 70, 77, 82, 92, 93, 126, 135, 140, 147, 151, 192, 206, 227, 228
consensus, 6, 8, 30, 139
control, 14, 16, 70, 72, 92, 120, 127, 176, 188, 192, 203, 225